Restaurant Winners

Plain Talk for Bootstrappers Navigating the Foodservice Industry

Mark Radford

© 2015 Mark Radford

ALL RIGHTS RESERVED. No part of this work covered by the copyright herein may be reproduced, transmitted, stored, or used in any form or by any means graphic, electronic, or mechanical, including but not limited to photocopying, recording, scanning, digitizing, taping, Web distribution, information networks, or information storage and retrieval systems, except as permitted under Section 107 or 108 of the 1976 United States Copyright Act, without the prior written permission of the publisher.

All trademarks are the property of their respective owners.

All images © Mark Radford unless otherwise noted.

Library of Congress Control Number: 2015916336

ISBN-13: (print) 978-0-692-51528-0

ISBN-13: (digital) 978-0-692-51529-7

ISBN-10: (print) 0692515283

ISBN-10: (digital) 0692515291

Printed in the United States of America

For all the fish and wing joints, BBQs, and bistros, fine dining and food trucks, caterers and concessionaires. For Erin, Nick, Hannah, Kathleen, Archie, and anybody who spent a nickel on our cooking.

Respectfully,

M.R.

Acknowledgments

I want to thank my brother-in-law, George Hanna of Canal Bistro, for the fateful phone call. Chef Allen Shideler, Jack Esselman, Chef James Jones of His Place Eatery, and Corey Smith for their participation. Many thanks to author Erik Deckers for the words of encouragement and my editor Kate Shoup.

About the Author

After spending 10 years in corporate America, **Mark Radford** left for entrepreneurial pursuits in foodservice, which have included concessions, catering, and quick-service restaurants. After nearly 20 years, he continues to be fascinated by all things related to foodservice, the restaurant business, and the people behind it.

Table of Contents

Introduction xiii

Chapter 1: How We Landed Here 1
    New Orleans 2
    New York City 2
    Back Home Again 3
    Ready for a Change 3
    Starting Small 4
    Giving Notice 6
    Finding a Kitchen 7
    The Next Phase 8
    Hard Times 10
    A Second Chance 11
    The Upshot 14

Chapter 2: Fair Warning 15
    Seduced By the Food Business 15
    It's Easier Than You Think 16
    It's Harder Than You Can Imagine 16
    The Bottom Line 18

Chapter 3: Choosing Your Business Model 19
    Catering 19
    Concessions 23
    Food Trucks 26

Opening a Restaurant	27
Private Chef	28

Chapter 4: A Sample Business Plan 31

What's in a Business Plan?	31
The Executive Summary	32
Mission and Strategy	32
Market	32
Pricing, Profitability, and Break-Even	32
Operations	34
Management and Staffing	34
Contingency Plans	34
Financial Projections	34
Repayment of Debt	34
A Sample Business Plan	35
In Closing...	43

Chapter 5: Getting Your Finances in Order 45

Cleaning Up Your Own House	45
Financing Your Operation	46
How Much Do You Need?	47

Chapter 6: Location, Location, Location 49

Choosing an Area	49
Downtown/CBD	49
Midtown	51
The "Downtown Donut"	52
The Suburbs	52

Assessing the Location 54

Should You Buy or Lease? 56

One Last Thing 57

Chapter 7: A Sample Timeline to Opening Day 63

When Should You Open? 63

24–12 Months to Opening Day 64

12–6 Months to Opening Day 65

    Choosing Your Food Vendors 66

    Mapping Out Your Kitchen 70

    Signing Up with a Bank and a Merchant Services Company 70

6–3 Months to Opening Day 71

    Building Out Your Space 71

    Narrowing Down Your Equipment List 72

    Creating Your Logo 73

    Shopping for Signage 73

3 Months to Opening Day 74

    Equipment 74

    Putting Your Kitchen Together 76

1 Month to Opening Day 77

1 Week to Opening Day 79

Opening Day 80

    What Day Should You Open? 81

    Making Sure You're Fully Stocked 81

    Making Sure You're Fully Staffed 82

    Taking Stock 82

Chapter 8: Hiring and Firing 85
Filling the Ranks 86
Do You Need a Manager? 87
Growing Your Staff 87
Your Labor Pool 88
Ignoring Stereotypes 90
Some of Our Brand Ambassadors 90
General Tips 92

Chapter 9: Marketing 93
Marketing Channels 93
Social Media 94
    Choosing Your Platform 95
    Who Should Handle Your Social Media? 95
    What Should You Share on Social Media? 96
    Don't Forget to Follow! 97
    Dealing with Customers on Social Media 98
E-mail Marketing 99
Guerilla Marketing 100
Creating Value Through Scarcity 101
To Discount or Not to Discount? 101
Do You Need a Marketing Company? 102

Chapter 10: The Pop 105
Our Pop 105
Dealing with It 108

Chapter 11: Your Guests 111

- You Are in the People Business 111
- Understanding Who's Who 112
- The Good, the Bad, and the Ugly 114
- Scammers and Hustlers 115
- Miscreants, Knaves, and Ne'er-Do-Wells 117

Chapter 12: Handling Criticism 121

- Niche-Based Criticism 122
- The "Write Stuff" 122
  - Food Writers 123
  - Restaurant Critics 123
  - Internet Reviewers 124
- Responding To (or Ignoring) Critics 125
- Hey! Our Place Was on TV! 128

Chapter 13: The People in Your World 129

- Delivery Drivers 129
- Repair Technicians 131
- Attorneys, Accountants, and Other Professionals 134
- Neighbors 135

Chapter 14: The Lifestyle 141

- First, the Bad News.... 141
- Now, the Good News! 142
- Setting Boundaries 143
- Cars, Clothes, and Money 144

Paying Yourself 146

Monopoly Money and Honeycomb Hideouts 147

Chapter 15: Things Fall Apart (The Lifestyle, Part II) 151

Dealing with Down Times 153

    Your P&L Statement..154

    A Sample Scenario 159

Keeping Up with Payments..161

    Paying Your Taxes...162

    Paying Vendors 162

    Paying Your Staff..162

    Paying Your Landlord 163

Closing Your Doors...164

Chapter 16: Moving, Expanding, and Selling.. 169

Moving the Business 169

Opening More Locations 173

Selling Your Business..174

Chapter 17: Dealing with Life Events 177

Chapter 18: If You Sell to Foodservice People 181

Make an Appointment 182

Tell Us About Changes Ahead of Time 182

Help Us Find Ways to Save..183

Chapter 19: To My Fellow Americans 187

The Power of Ownership 187

The American Dream 188

Chapter 20: Leftovers 191
Enjoying the Challenge 191
Snobbery 191
Making Do in Flyover Country 192
Our Indy 193
Cooking for Fun 194
Our Wish for You 194

Introduction

Everybody knows the foodservice business is difficult. Nevertheless, restaurants and caterers make an obscene amount of money. The amount of money they spend, however, is equally obscene. What's left over goes to the owner. This book is about whether that amount is enough to make owning a foodservice business worth the life that comes with it. If you decide this world is for you, you need to assess your threshold for risk as well as how much of yourself you want to give—because this business asks for a lot.

My wife Erin and I have been in the industry nearly twenty years and so far, we have survived without the help of banks, investors, or partners. For us, owning a foodservice business is worth it. We enjoy the perks and freedom that come with owning our own business and the dynamic nature of the restaurant industry. This book offers a look at how you, too, can start your own foodservice business—on your own terms—and survive.

Maybe you picked up this book because you're ready to open your first food business. Maybe you're a veteran of the industry and want to enjoy a trip down memory lane. Whoever you are, I'm confident there's value in these pages for you. For too many years, my wife and I have watched our peers come and go—and far more quickly than they should have. We've also seen experienced operators flush hundreds of thousands of dollars down the toilet in a matter of months and witnessed accomplished, intelligent people walk into the ass end of a losing situation...not once, not twice, but multiple times. And then repeat this behavior. We want to help you avoid this.

We'll share with you how we got in the restaurant business, what worked, what didn't, and what we would do differently if given the chance. That being said, what worked for us may not work for you—and vice versa. Although there are some best practices in this industry, there are no hard and fast rules. There's no right or wrong way other than making the numbers fit. I won't bore you with complex equations and mathematical formulas, however, because the math involved is quite simple.

The title is *Restaurant Winners* because we want you to win in the foodservice industry. Simply opening a business is not winning. Being in business and being profitable is winning. Being in business and breaking even is half-winning. Being in business and losing doesn't make sense. We'll cover as much as we can to put you in the best position possible to win while considering the most economic approach to do so.

In this book, I stick to what I know. I tell you where, in my opinion, the bulk of the money is made and lost by newcomers. I also introduce you to a few other people in the industry so they can share their knowledge. I won't discuss how to win in the bar business because I've never worked in that business and at present have no plans to do so. My focus here is on casual catering, concessions, and the quick-service concept—businesses with relatively low barriers to entry, which are the easiest to start on a small budget. The good thing is that you can apply the knowledge gained in these segments to more sophisticated ventures down the road if you so choose. Also, I'm not here to make a case for what you should serve and who you should serve it to, or to get into any stuffy, esoteric ramblings on culinary opinion. Your ideas can be as basic or complex as your imagination.

Foodservice is the most fascinating, frustrating, and rewarding business around, and you have the right to pursue your vision of it. It's being done every day by people just like you and me. I hope I can help answer some of your questions. Thanks for reading!

Chapter 1

How We Landed Here

Bear with me for a few pages and I'll explain what led to this book.

It is said people choose a career in foodservice for one of three reasons: new beginnings, second chances, or last resorts. For me—the first time, anyway—it was a new beginning. I worked in corporate America for almost 10 years, and that was enough to realize I'd be happier and do better financially by pursuing the goal of working for myself.

Ever since high school, I had known that at some point in my life, I wanted to own my own business. I had no idea I'd be cooking, though. I wasn't called to be a chef. I didn't begin my career washing dishes in restaurants at age 12. I'm not professionally trained in the culinary arts. In truth, growing up in my hometown, Indianapolis, during the 1970s and 1980s, there weren't many culinary standouts to inspire much of anyone into the cooking profession. It was, and still is, a meat-and-potatoes type of town (although that's changing). Back in those days, people mainly cooked at home. Meals were of the traditional, comfort-food variety. Sunday dinner was a big thing, with hearty selections of fried chicken, meatloaf, roasts, and anything barbequed, grilled, or baked.

Backyard gardens were as commonplace in my Indiana neighborhood as basketball hoops. We also had a number of pear and crab apple trees, with a few mulberry and cherry trees mixed in. Plus, we had easy access to wholesale meat shops, where you could buy a half cow or hog, whole chickens, slab bacon, and anything else you can imagine.

New Orleans

I didn't develop a hard-core appreciation for food until I left for college in New Orleans. There, I saw the zeal with which people in the South regard food. Northerners settled into our dorm rooms with mini fridges stuffed with bologna and cheese sandwiches or Mom's chocolate chip cookies. Meanwhile, the Southern kids brought hot plates, skillets, utensils, and seasonings. Walking through the hallways on any given weekend, you'd smell the spiciest, aromatic concoctions these resourceful college students could devise. Almost every week in the spring, fraternities and sororities held impromptu crawfish and crab boils in the park. Even the school cafeteria had decent food and kept local traditions: red beans and rice on Mondays, fish and spaghetti on Fridays, grits at breakfast seven days a week. Things were even better off campus. As I explored my new city, I tasted boudin, turtle, and various étouffées, gumbos, and bisques. This sparked in me a serious interest in good food and learning how to cook it.

New York City

After college I went back home and spent a couple uneventful years working in insurance when an opportunity arrived. I landed a job in medical sales with a company I'll call Megapharm. My territory was Brooklyn, New York—not today's kinder, gentrified borough, but the gritty, rough and tough early '90s Brooklyn. I really looked forward to working in a city I'd grown up hearing so much about. Although the job was in Brooklyn, I lived in Manhattan, renting an apartment from an aunt who owned a brownstone in Harlem. For the next three years, I made the daily trip into my territory via the FDR. After working in Brooklyn all day, I drove back to the city and enjoyed all that came with living in Manhattan. It was a wonderful time.

The food culture in New York City is nothing short of amazing. It would take a person years to eat at all the places worth trying. I ate at Senegalese restaurants and Jewish delis, Trinidadian roti shops, Korean barbeque places, American soul food joints, Jamaican vegetarian spots, Italian trattorias—you name it, I ate it. Sometimes I explored these places on my own. Many times it was courtesy of my expense account with Megapharm. You see, being successful in medical sales means gaining the undivided attention of decision makers. With medical professionals, this is no small task. They are busy people. Often, the best—and sometimes the only—way to get their undivided attention is over a meal. So Megapharm spent mind-blowing amounts of money on these outings. In most cases, we hit high-end restaurants in Brooklyn, Queens, or Manhattan. Expensive bottles of wine, single-malt scotches, and champagne

Chapter 1: How We Landed Here

flowed together to accompany fabulous gourmet meals—with Megapharm footing the bill. These were regular outings, often several times a week. The point of the whole affair was relationship building, with the hope that when it came time for the doctor to put pen to pad, it would *my* products they remembered and prescribed. For me, it opened up a world I'd never been exposed to with respect to food and drink and how much of the world's business is done at the dinner table.

Back Home Again

It was on a trip home in August for my 10th high-school reunion that I realized my days in New York were numbered. I'm an only child. My parents divorced when I was six, and I was raised by my mother and grandfather. Sadly, my mother struggled for years with serious depression. At the time of my visit, she had her hands full with my grandfather, who was 90 years old and had the age-related health issues you'd expect. When I got into town and looked around, I knew what time it was. The house was in terrible shape. The grass was up to my knees. My mother, as was her M.O., never maintained her car, so it constantly broke down. Things were going downhill fast. Although I had a great job in my dream city, the writing was on the wall. In my book, family is first, so I decided that when I got back from my trip, I'd request a transfer to Indianapolis. And miraculously, by Thanksgiving, I was back home.

My grandfather passed away exactly one year and one month after my return. Things were somewhat of a mess back home financially, so I spent the next several years bailing my mother out of one situation after the next. At the same time, I was also dealing with my own divorce. I quickly found myself stuck in a funk between that, missing my grandfather, and worrying about my mother. And to be honest, my career was going nowhere. Although I had been with Megapharm for going on eight years, I essentially started over with the transfer back home. And being on my fourth manager certainly didn't help with any advancement opportunities. I was ready to move on but had no idea what to do next. The one bright spot was meeting my new girlfriend, Erin.

Ready for a Change

My job with Megapharm in Indy was more or less the same as in New York, but with one significant twist. When working in New York, gaining access to doctors meant taking them out to a nice dinner. In Indy, the best way gain access to these professionals was to bring in lunch for their whole office—sometimes 30 or more people! One day, after finishing another routine sales presentation at a physician's office, I was alone in the break room, putting away my sales materials. I took a long look at the lunch I had brought in from a local caterer—the gummy lasagna, the picked-over iceberg salad, and what was left of the chocolate chip cookies. I also took notice of a bagel and cream cheese breakfast another rep had brought in that morning. Next to it was a basket of wet naps, presumably from a barbeque lunch earlier that week, as well as a bunch of those little packets of parmesan cheese and red pepper flakes you get with pizza deliveries.

How much food had been brought into this office in the last few days? Up until then, I'd never really paid attention. Then I looked at the receipt from my caterer. The meal I'd brought in cost $300. I quickly did the math. I was spending between $2,000 and $3,000 per month on breakfasts and lunches—and there were five other Megapharm reps in my territory alone doing the exact same thing. And we weren't the only ones. In addition to Megapharm, there were 10 or 15 other pharmaceutical companies with reps in our territory—all using caterers every day of the week.

"I'll be damned," I thought.

Right then and there, I had my answer as to what my next move was: a catering business. Hell, I could make box lunches, chicken Caesar salads, and tuna salad wraps! And having more or less lived as a caterer by day and a restaurant host by night, I felt I knew what good service looked like. Plus, after eating, drinking, and generally hanging out in hundreds of restaurants for the last seven or eight years, I'd put my palate up against any food critic.

I thought about it some more: I spent $300 on one office that day. If I catered only three lunches per week, I'd pull in $900. What if I catered three per day—or more? The more I thought about it, the more it made sense. I got mad at myself for not putting two and two together years earlier.

Up until then, I had zero experience cooking for pay. Nor did I have entrepreneurial experience (except for cutting grass as a teenager). But it was decided. I was going to open a catering business.

Starting Small

I started small. Rather than abruptly leaving Megapharm's safety net, I catered on the side. I figured I'd try my hand at it for a few months to see how it went. That way, if it wasn't for me, at least I'd still have a job.

Chapter 1: How We Landed Here

I didn't go it alone. With Erin's help, I set about getting everything together from an administrative standpoint—filing paperwork with the state, obtaining a business checking account, and so on. (More on that later.) I was ready to start making money, but needed two things to get started: customers and a place to make the food.

Getting customers wasn't hard. Some friends in medical sales were kind enough to let me test run on scheduled lunches with their offices. Plus, Erin—who was also a pharmaceutical rep—gave me everything on her calendar. No one at Megapharm knew what I was I was doing and I wasn't stupid enough to cater my own lunches with Megapharm's money, which would've meant automatic termination. My only risk of discovery was running into another Megapharm rep while dropping off lunch somewhere.

In terms of the food, everything was simple and familiar: deli sandwiches, chips, slaw or potato salad, fruit and cheese trays, and a few easy pasta dishes, along with some entrée salads. Beverages were two-liter bottles of soda sent with bagged ice. Usually, I brought brownies or cookies for dessert. Plates, cups, napkins, and plastic ware were included, and everything was disposable, so the jobs were always a one way, drop-off-and-leave scenario.

I didn't reinvent the wheel. I just followed the model of the successful caterers I'd been using all those years. There was no need to overthink what had already worked for dozens of businesses. The goal in our case was just to make everything look and taste a little better. Why not have fresh-cut fruit in an attractive black bowl, with some thinly sliced limes and mint leaves for a garnish? How about using multi-colored and flavored wraps instead of plain white ones for a nice punch of color? This was what we were going for.

Still, it wasn't easy. After about a month of stumbling and bumbling, being late with deliveries, and begging for second chances, I quickly grasped that a key challenge pertained to space. When cooking for large groups, there simply isn't enough room in a regular, residential refrigerator. Immediately, I purchased a used reach-in commercial cooler. (The challenge after that was how to move it into the kitchen of the duplex I lived in.)

Another key challenge was time. There is never enough time in the kitchen. Worse, what seems like an easy lasagna and salad lunch for 20 people can quickly turn into a nightmare if your timing is off in the slightest. I learned the hard way to allow for cook times, packaging, and travel.

Eventually, I felt more relaxed and comfortable, and by the second month, things started to get easier and to fire on all cylinders. I listened to feedback from Erin and my customers and got better at being organized, managing portions, and getting out the door.

After just eight weeks, I had managed about $7,000 in sales, working a few hours a day, two or three days a week. Even buying everything retail, there was a damn good profit. Plus, I'd landed a weekend concession job that had netted another $2,800.

After that, my mind was made up. I was leaving Megapharm and pursuing foodservice full time. The numbers were too good to keep working a corporate job.

It wasn't just the money that was attractive. It was the feeling that I could do something for myself—something I enjoyed. And of course, it was a new beginning. I desperately needed a reset and realized if I didn't make a move now, I probably never would. Erin came on board as a partner of sorts. She would help me get the new business up and running, but the initial financial investment would be all on me.

> **NOTE**
>
> There was one problem with my operation in its earliest incarnation: Technically, it was illegal. Simply put, if you're preparing and selling food to the public, the county health department requires you to have a license. This license is granted only after you pass an inspection of the commercial kitchen or commissary where everything is made. (There are exceptions for certain homemade foods. If you think your operation might qualify, consult with your local authorities to find out more.) Because I was preparing food in my home, I was in violation of this rule. I don't suggest you do this, however. These days, there are commercial kitchens you can lease on a per-use basis. Some churches also lease their kitchens out for commissary use. Had this option been available to me at the time, I would have taken it, and I advise you to do the same.

Giving Notice

In June of that year I sent an e-mail to my manager, announcing my resignation effective immediately. We followed that up with a pleasant phone conversation. He asked me what I was planning to do. I told him a positive step toward some personal goals. All that was left was for me to return my drug samples, turn in the company vehicle, and tie up a few loose ends. After a week, it was over. I'd done it. I'd quit.

Chapter 1: How We Landed Here

Two weeks later, I reflected on what I'd done. In my haste to leave, I hadn't considered how many unresolved financial issues I had. I quit without paying off credit cards and other debt, including student loans. Plus, there was the mortgage on the duplex I'd bought a few years earlier—a fixer-upper near downtown. Part of that was offset by a tenant, but it still needed major repairs, including new HVAC, windows, and a roof.

The good news was I had a healthy 401k. When I quit, there was roughly $70,000, split between Megapharm stock and some aggressive mutual funds. The bad news was I'd take a hit when I withdrew from it. Still, I took comfort in the fact it was there if I needed it. Shortly after resigning, the Megapharm stock (and the market in general) had a nice run, and my nest egg grew to $90,000. (Sadly, I would see all of it evaporate in about a year.)

Finding a Kitchen

They say God looks out for fools and babies. That proved true for me when, about three months later, we found a commercial kitchen to lease. (I stopped catering from home once I quit Megapharm. No need to risk getting into trouble downtown. But I languished at home paying bills with no income until we found it!)

The space was located near the corner of two busy streets in an historic neighborhood just north of downtown. Tiny—maybe 900 square feet—it was in the basement of a three-story walkup that once housed a popular local sandwich shop. The landlords rented it to us for $500 a month on a year-to-year basis. Erin didn't like it so much, but that didn't matter. She still had regular-paying a job. I was thrilled. I thought it was a great location, and only 10 minutes from my house to boot. We signed the lease and went about setting up shop.

The kitchen area comprised about a third of the space, separated from the dining room by a short hallway with small restrooms—about the size you'd find in an airplane—on either side. The remainder of the area was then divided into three even smaller spaces. The largest of these had room for a desk, a convection oven, an ice machine, and the reach-in cooler I brought from my house. The room next to it contained a five-foot-long sandwich prep table, miniature freezer, two-bay sink, and small stainless steel prep table. In the back room was a narrow galley-like area, which contained a three bay bar sink and a wire shelf for pans and utensils. The back door opened to an alley, which was convenient for loading orders into a waiting car or van. The whole place sat underground, though, and it was a bitch to move equipment up and down the stairs. Plus, it flooded after any heavy rainstorm, and the only parking available to us was a single space across the street in the landlord's private parking lot. Still, we had found a home. I hired a manager and another cook to help me out and we got rolling.

Admittedly, things started slow. Apart from a few friends keeping me afloat, I didn't get much in the way of orders for the first few weeks. Eventually, though, things got moving. I'll never forget when the first legit order came from a complete stranger. It was a traveling sales rep who ordered box lunches for 10 people delivered to an electrical contractor's office. I took the call myself, and was so nervous, my hands shook as I wrote the order down.

More orders came, and after a year, we were busy enough to have outgrown the space. We bought a vacated auto-body shop about two miles north in a rough but mostly quiet residential/light industrial area. It had a private office with a bathroom, concrete floors, a huge three-phase electrical panel, and security bars on the windows. To meet code for a commercial kitchen, we installed a drop ceiling and put in sinks and a grease trap. At a cool 2,700 square feet with a mortgage around $700 per month, it was a good move. We still had a good location, and now we had our own parking lot and a small fenced-in yard as well.

We added more items to our deli-centric menu, like French toast and quiche Lorraine along with some additional pasta and stir-fry dishes. The focus was healthy eating, so everything was either raw, baked, sautéed, or roasted.

The Next Phase

We grew the business for three more years, did some side concession work for a time, and built up a strong client base. In our opinion, it was a successful run.

The focus was mostly corporate catering, so I worked Monday through Friday, starting around 6 a.m. and ending at noon. I had weekends and holidays off because most businesses were closed on those days, although every now and then we did private parties on Saturdays. We learned as we went and had a ball.

I estimate the business netted around $45,000 or $50,000 a year—about the same as my base at Megapharm. But there was no credit-card debt, my vehicle was paid for, I worked fewer than 30 hours a week, and I enjoyed all the tax advantages of being a business owner. After the fourth year, however, we decided it was time to sell, for a variety of reasons.

For one thing, although catering was great, I spent a lot of time waiting on checks. At first, this was no big deal. But eventually, it became unnerving waiting 60 or 90 days to

Chapter 1: How We Landed Here

get paid. Erin and I got married and had a son and realized that when you're starting a family, having a guaranteed income, like Erin still had, is a crucial factor in responsible living—and having two guaranteed incomes is even better. If I went back to work full time, we could live off one and save the other, I could get paid vacations again, and if something ever happened with Erin's job, we'd have a plan B that was a little more solid than just the catering operation.

For another thing, it was a good time to sell. There was increasing competition from corporate chain restaurants cashing in on office and private catering. It was becoming difficult to compete on price, and we couldn't offer all the bells and whistles a well-heeled brand provided. In addition, our pharmaceutical clientele was thinning out, as companies had been pulling back expense budgets for the last few years.

It was a good time to move on. We learned a lot, the business stayed solvent, and besides, we could always do it again if we wanted to.

In January of what would be our last year, we listed the business for sale with a broker. At the same time, I updated my resume and hit the bricks looking for another job in pharma, the only thing I knew other than food. I knew it wouldn't be easy, but with almost five years running my own business and managing people, and a solid performance at Megapharm before that, I thought I'd be a shoe-in for senior-level field sales or maybe even a district manager position.

I was in for a rude awakening. Nobody gave two shits about any of it. The few interviews that came my way put me in competition with anxious and moldable 20-somethings who were willing to relocate, travel the state, and accept at least $30,000 less than what I thought I was worth. The fact was, I was five years out of the game, there weren't many new products to sell, and companies were beginning to downsize.

Finally, in August, we hit pay dirt. We found a buyer for our business, including the real estate we were selling with it. (I would regret that for a long time. We should have kept the building.) And I got a job offer. It wasn't exactly what I hoped for, but it was work and a steady paycheck. And even though it was a complete 180 from the Wall Street giant I'd come from, it was actually rather refreshing. There was a modest expense budget for lunches, but there were no fancy dinners or plane rides to resort hotels for meetings, which was fine by me. All that mattered was getting back into the industry. The end game was to crank out the numbers with this outfit and seek out a bigger company to eventually land at. I was back in the hard-to-crack medical sales club, and that was all I needed—or so I thought.

Hard Times

About a year after I started that job, we became proud parents of a baby girl. Around the same time, I began another job search. To my dismay, not much had changed. If anything, my prospects had grown worse. Think about it: I left Megapharm in New York to move to Indy. I left Megapharm in Indy to be a caterer. I left catering to work for a small startup. And now I was trying to leave them to go work somewhere else.

Unsurprisingly, I never did land that next job. Worse, 18 months in, I was fired from the job I had. Maybe they were thinning the herd for a merger that eventually came. Maybe my territory didn't generate enough dollars. Whatever the reason, I was told to grab my hat. It was a blow, but at least Erin still had her job. Besides, I was sure I'd get something else going.

Six weeks after I got fired, Erin lost her job, too. Why? Who knows. In an employment-at-will state, like Indiana is, you can be fired for any reason (or for no reason). Maybe it was because she and her manager had never had the coziest of relationships. Possibly, it was because she, like me, had committed the crime of approaching her late 30s. It's odd—pharmaceutical sales is one of the few professions where your worth actually goes *down* the longer you're in it. Accountants, attorneys, and doctors usually earn higher wages the longer they're in their professions. Not so in pharma. After all, the thinking goes, what can someone in her late 30s do that a 25-year-old can't?

Anyway, it didn't matter. We were in deep shit. Two incomes and all associated benefits were gone. We were both almost 40 years old, with the majority of our work experience in an industry in which we were considered obsolete. And of course, we had two kids under three years old.

We filed for unemployment and got on the dole but felt no shame in it. The way we saw it, we'd paid into the system all our working lives, so we were just getting back our own money. Still, it was humbling to say the least.

We sent out resumes, networked, answered ads, and did everything else we could to find work, but nothing happened. Fortunately, even though the catering business wiped out all my savings, we weren't completely destitute. Erin had her 401k and I still had my duplex rental. But we knew time was ticking and that the money would run out eventually.

Chapter 1: How We Landed Here

A Second Chance

It was late December, 2006. Erin and I had been out of work for nearly six months. Both of us were stressed from being jobless and watching our savings disappear. Worse, our unemployment—which barely covered our mortgages and daycare—was due to expire in a few weeks.

With my back against the wall, I had applied for a second-shift part-time job with Federal Express as a package handler. I passed the lift test and other screenings and was just waiting on a call back. Erin was having less luck. She received not one but *two* rejection letters from Von Maur for an ordinary retail sales position. It took them half a page to tell her she was overqualified, but thanked her for her interest.

One evening, I was shoveling snow at my mother's house. As I made my way down the sidewalk tossing the heavy, wet snow into the yard, my phone rang. It was Erin.

"Hey," she said. "I just got off the phone with my brother. He wants to know if you still want to do that burger joint you talked about. He knows some guys selling a restaurant, and it's in a great spot."

Way back, before the kids were born, Erin and I enjoyed traveling around the country. We especially enjoyed eating at neighborhood greasy spoons and at the burger and taco stands that dotted the California coast. To this day, if we're in a new town, those are the places we seek out first. We kicked around the idea of one day having one of those places back in Indy—a small space with a few chairs and maybe somewhere to eat outside. We'd have grilled burgers, chicken, maybe a veggie or fish option, and milkshakes. Our version would include the traditional cheeseburger but with some interesting toppings. Everything would be cooked on a broiler, there'd be an open kitchen so guests could see the flames lick up from the grates, and the wonderful aroma would waft down the block. We even put together a binder with a sample menu, notes on what we'd seen and liked at different places, and other ideas, but it had been gathering dust on a shelf for the last five years.

Still, I wasn't interested in cooking again. I grunted a "Nah" and told her I needed to hang up so I could finish Mom's sidewalk. But when I got home, Erin wouldn't let it go—and I'm glad she didn't.

We evaluated our situation. Our unemployment was about to run out, and we had a $3,000 nut on daycare and mortgages alone. Yes, I was likely to get the part-time job at

FedEx. But after taxes and deductions, it wouldn't do more than pay for gas money to get back and forth to work. For her part, Erin still had no job and no real prospects.

The way we saw it, we had two obvious options. The first was to grind out whatever jobs we could get and make the wages work as best we could. But frankly, that seemed like no way to live. The second option was to check out this restaurant for sale and try our burger joint idea. Even though we had never operated a quick-service restaurant, we didn't think it could be that hard. We'd done concessions for a few years along with the catering; the burger joint would basically be a concession tent, except with a real roof over our heads, tables, and a bathroom. After much consideration, we realized this was our best option, so we contacted the seller and agreed to meet him at the restaurant the following week.

On a cold weeknight in January, we went to look at the restaurant. We were familiar with the spot—a cottage-like structure that sat near a corner in a popular neighborhood. Its current incarnation was a quick-service gyro joint. There were three or four bar tables squeezed into a roughly 200-square-foot dining room and a counter that ran the length of two sides of the room—about 13 seats in all. A huge picture window faced the sidewalk.

The story on the place was interesting. Originally, it had been the kitchen for a restaurant next door. Between the two properties was a patio, which seated around 80 people. At the south side of the patio was a hallway that connected the two buildings. Everything for the restaurant was made in the shack of a kitchen and then run down the hallway into the restaurant or onto the patio. The restaurant had closed a few years earlier but remained open as a bar. Subsequently, the hallway between the restaurant and the kitchen was sealed off, and the kitchen was cleverly converted into a walk-up food stand with patio access.

On the other side of the kitchen was a renowned local steakhouse with a 20 year history, located in a 100-year-old historic building. Down the street was a family-owned Italian restaurant that had been around for more than 30 years. It was a great block in a thriving area, but for whatever reason, nothing was working in this little space for sale.

So what was the deal with the gyro operation? After a few minutes of talking with the owner, we got the picture. It had been started by three or four people looking to make some easy cash. They had only been in business a little over 12 weeks, but after long days and nights with just enough coming in to pay bills and payroll—and the fact that they were now facing the coldest and slowest months, January and February—they realized it wasn't worth the trouble. Although the restaurant was still limping along,

Chapter 1: How We Landed Here

the group had smartly made the decision to cut and run. All they wanted was to get back what they put into it, so they were selling the business and equipment, along with the assumption of their lease, for $60,000. Take it or leave it.

Of course we had no interest in the business. We were after the already-built-out and furnished restaurant space and location. The truth was, we were hot on the space. The fact that the gyro shop failed—as had another concept before it—didn't concern us in the least. If we did it right, we thought, that little shack could be a banger. It was perfect for something like a burger stand.

The problem was we didn't want to pay anywhere near the number they were asking. We were out of cash and would have to tap Erin's 401k. I remembered how quickly I burned through almost $100,000 in a single year with the catering business—and this would be a much riskier. Out of the gate, we'd need more labor and have to keep a larger inventory. Plus, because most of what they were selling was unusable for our concept, we needed about $5,000 worth of equipment.

The only way to get the space without buying out the owners of the gyro shop would be to wait until they went out of business and be first in line when the "For Lease" sign went up in the window. The problem with that strategy was twofold. First, we were running out of time. We needed to get something going right away, as our unemployment was ending in about two weeks. The owners of the gyro shop could hold out longer than we could. Second, if we waited, there was no guarantee we'd get the space. Someone else could come along and pay the asking price. Even if that didn't happen, there might already be a waiting list for the property when they closed up shop.

We knew our city well enough to know there wouldn't be a similar space, at that rent, at that location, anytime soon—if ever. It was shit or get off the pot. So we gritted our teeth, withdrew $60,000 from Erin's 401k, and paid up.

The decision to get back into foodservice was our proverbial jump shot with one second on the clock, but it turned out to be the biggest return on any investment we'd ever made up to that point.

We were an early entry into the burgeoning "better burger" segment when we opened four months later. Eventually, there would be a line out of the door and down the sidewalk. The patio space we leased from the bar was packed full every weekend. After four years bursting at the seams, we would move, setting up shop in a bigger space down the street. And over the years, we'd sell millions of dollars of our food. Foodservice had come to the rescue.

The Upshot

We made plenty of mistakes along the way, and we continue to learn right up to the present. But we did it, and you can too.

Maybe you're in a state of flux or at the end of your rope like we were. Maybe you're financially secure but you have an idea you just have to try because you *know* it will work. Either way, you're ready—but the thought of getting from here to there makes your head spin. Read on, and I'll share how we've survived it.

Chapter 2

Fair Warning

Recently, I ran into a guy who had been a sales rep for a food vendor. We were both shopping in one of those restaurant-supply warehouses. The last time I'd seen him, about 18 months prior, he was about to open his own restaurant—which he eventually did to rave reviews. As we stood by our heavy gray metal carts—his full of pork loins and mine with fresh mushrooms, lettuce, and serrano chilies—I congratulated him on his incredible launch. But I couldn't help but notice he had "the look"—the obvious weariness that comes from working long hours. Based on his success, it was clear he was on his way to living the dream. But his obvious fatigue reminded me this isn't for the faint of heart. It got me to thinking about the truth about the food business: It's easier than you think…yet harder than you can imagine.

Seduced By the Food Business

Who doesn't dream of owning a restaurant? A fast-paced, lively social hub, filled with a variety of guests coming and going. A place where there's laughter at the bar, where important deals go down at out-of-the-way tables during lunch. People flocking to your place for an opportunity to relax and enjoy themselves. First dates, birthdays, anniversaries—they're all part of the fun.

If you were the owner of such an establishment, you'd likely enjoy a bit of local fame, a respectable cash flow, and if it matters to you, your name and picture in the paper from time to time. You'd be a contributor to the cultural fabric of your neighborhood and city. Not only that, but you'd have the autonomy to direct, control, and make decisions that come with owning your own business.

Foodservice is a multi-billion-dollar business that stays up more than down. I'd argue that after prostitution, foodservice is the *second* oldest profession—and it is never going away. After all, as long as you're alive, you gotta eat! Even better, it has a sales cycle that takes place in seconds or minutes, not weeks or months. In this industry, you close deals—hundreds of them—every day. And every day, you receive immediate payment, often amounting to thousands of dollars.

Who wouldn't be seduced?

It's Easier Than You Think

At its base, the food business—like many other businesses—is quite simple. You buy and resell. In doing so, you gain customers and you lose customers (although I prefer the term *guests*). The trick is to keep more than you lose and always attract new business. (Now, I could end the book right there, but obviously there's more to it than that.)

It's Harder Than You Can Imagine

Before you even think about launching your own foodservice business, you'll want to have an honest conversation with yourself about the new life you plan on undertaking. Here are just a few of the challenges you're likely to face:

- There will be no more paid vacations or holidays.
- Work will not end at 5 o'clock or even 10 o'clock.
- You will work weekends. They're the busiest days.
- Fridays will feel like Mondays.

During your honest conversation, ask yourself these questions:

- What will you do about medical, dental, and life insurance?
- Are you married?
- Do you have kids? If so, how old are they?
- How old are *you*? Are you in your 30s, 40s, or 50s?
- How's your health?
- Are you going it alone or will you need partners?
- Will you be open seven days a week?
- Have you managed people before?
- What competition is already out there?
- What niches are you going after—casual dining, quick service, or upscale? Restaurant, catering, concessions, or food truck?
- Do you have enough cash to get started?
- What's your exit strategy if things don't work out?

Chapter 2: Fair Warning

You'll also want to consider these unfortunate realities:

- You may spend thousands of dollars on new kitchen equipment and furniture that's worth pennies on the dollar if you go out of business.
- You could be on the hook for the eight-year balance left on a 10-year lease.
- You might lose your entire 401k and any money you've pulled out of your house.
- The business could affect your marriage.
- You might pick up unhealthy addictions while dealing with the stress involved in keeping the place running and profitable.
- Your business will be criticized—and the majority of people do not take criticism well.
- Your employees *and* guests will steal from you.
- You'll deal with the embarrassment of not being able to pay your bills on time.
- You will deal with jealousy and envy.

All this explains why, when people tell me they're thinking of opening a restaurant, my reaction is a combination of genuine excitement and compassionate alarm. I can't help but wonder to myself whether the $50,000, $80,000, or $300,000 they're about to spend would be better invested someplace else, like real estate or the stock market. I can't help but wonder if they know about the long hours required, about the days fraught with worry for a business that is likely to fail, and the piles of debt they'll likely amass along the way.

And I'm not the only one who wonders that. Anyone who's been in the food business wonders the same thing. That's why so many—including me—discourage the majority of people from entering the industry. Trust me: It's not that we're afraid of competition. It's that we know you have to be built a certain way to survive in this business—and most people aren't. We also know that most food businesses fail. Out of 10 people we talk to, only three will actually follow through and open something. Out of the three, one will close in a short time. The second will struggle until the owners tire and eventually shut their doors. The third will stay open and be profitable over the years. We want to save you some pain!

One thing I can tell you is this: The food is the easiest part. If you make great barbeque or tuna fish salad and think people will buy it, they probably will. The key to longevity turns on two simple things: Dealing with people and the basic use of a calculator.

> **CAUTION**
>
> If you choose to embark on this journey, don't let TV food personalities, cookbook authors, or the latest celebrity chefs influence your decision-making processes. I respect what they do and share their passion for food, but unless they've owned and operated something that depends on real people walking through the doors and sitting at the tables, you'll gain a lot more by talking with your favorite hot dog cart operator or the owner of the neighborhood diner that has been open for 30 years.

The Bottom Line

Hopefully I've scared off all the bullshitters and half-steppers. By now, I'm guessing there are two types of people still reading: those who want no part in this insanity and those who can't wait for the punishment but eventual rewards the business can bring. Sometimes.

Here's the deal: If you absolutely cannot sleep at night thinking about your idea, if you are honest with yourself about what it takes to succeed, and if you have a strong work ethic, then this business may be a great fit for you. True, it is difficult, but it's not impossible. You can win at this game with some planning and common sense.

> **NOTE**
>
> Often, it's a journey *just to get to the decision* to make a go of this business. Whatever you do, don't rush. Maybe you're a year out, maybe three. Don't worry. Whenever you jump in, there will be room for you. Places open and close on a daily basis. If you've made up your mind to take it seriously, put the work in, and go for it, congratulations and welcome! If you choose to stay the hell out, we understand! Either way, you'll be helping the industry.

Chapter 3

Choosing Your Business Model

If you've decided to start your own foodservice business, what type of operation do you want? You have a few choices:

- Catering
- Concession
- Food truck
- Restaurant (full or quick-service)

All of these options can make money, just as they can lose money. The option you choose depends on which one makes the best use of your skills and abilities. It also depends on what you can offer in terms of time and money. In the end, it comes down to your risk tolerance. Ask yourself, if you invest a ton of money and years of your life, what is that worth to you? If you leave a job making, say, $60,000 a year to run your own business making half that, will that constitute a win? Only you can answer that.

> **NOTE**
> Looking back, we were able to make the most with the least doing catering. Concessions enabled us to make an incredible amount of money in a short period of time—although that was seasonal. And the restaurant has enabled us to stay in business the longest.

Catering

Catering is probably the least sexy member of the foodservice family. It's a clandestine operation of sorts, often operating from B real estate in out-of-the-way places. Most likely, the general public doesn't know who owns the top catering businesses in town, nor do they care. I doubt if anyone even could name three local caterers off the top of their head. You never read about grand openings for new catering companies. I'm guessing the only time a caterer penetrates your consciousness is when you see one of its vans or trucks zipping around town or when you casually ask "Who did the food?" at whatever events you attend. They go about their business, keeping a low profile, all while quietly raking in millions of dollars a year.

Professional caterers may or may not rank on the "cool" meter amongst restaurant chefs, mixologists, and local and national celebrity food folk, but one thing I can tell you is it doesn't matter. I can also tell you more than half the people we knew who were catering during the time we did it (2000–2005) are still in business, while less than 10% (if that) of the independent restaurants that opened during that time are still around.

Why is catering a great option? There are several reasons:

- It enables you to *ease* into the foodservice business. This is especially handy if you aren't starting with a lot of capital.
- You don't have to hold a lot of inventory, but you still learn the nuts and bolts of purchasing.
- You don't need a lot of employees—at least, not at first. Your initial staff may be only one or two people. And because these employees don't deal with the public (other than deliveries or answering the phone), they're easier to manage.
- It's quick, easy money. With catering, a few hours of work can pay in the hundreds or thousands.
- You don't have to deal with the pressure of a busy dining room and people coming and going.
- Unlike restaurants, which are generally open 10 or more hours a day, seven days a week, a caterer can work Monday through Friday or weekends and special events only. If all you do is cater breakfast and lunch for businesses, the hours are even shorter and the labor costs even more manageable.

Perhaps the most important reason is that with catering, you always know what's coming in ahead of time. If your bookings say you have to feed 200 people on Monday, 300 on Tuesday, 70 on Wednesday, none on Thursday, and 30 on Friday, it makes managing food costs so much easier. Until you go big time, there's no need to hold much inventory because it constantly flips. In contrast, if you're running a restaurant, you may have 50 people walk in one day, and 500 the next. Either way, you're expected to be adequately staffed and have everything available on the menu.

Chapter 3: Choosing Your Business Model

> **TIP**
> If you are brand new to the food business, don't have much money to risk, and want to keep the number of hands in your project at a minimum, consider catering. It allows a flexible schedule you can live with. From there, you can do just about anything.

So if you go the catering route, who's your customer? Anybody with a mouth, that's who! Corporate Offices and the salespeople who call on them are a good start. Car dealerships, insurance companies, brokerage and law firms, call centers, medical offices—any and all places where people want food brought in at some time or other. People hosting parties at event venues or in their homes but don't want to cook call their trusty caterer. We even interviewed with a regional airline that was looking for a caterer to provide box lunches for its daily flights. There are also business models based purely on home delivery of prepared food.

> **NOTE**
> Oddly, with catering, the bigger the group, the less food you have to make. There's something about seeing food *en masse* that makes most people eat less. Where a restaurant with 100 covers means having enough food for 100 people, a catering job for 100 people maybe requires you to make enough food for only 75 (but still charge for 100).

Catering isn't all roses, however. The competition is very intense. The surviving mom-and-pop caterers have grown into a comfortable space and are well connected with their clients. And just about every casual or quick-service chain has a catering arm with deep pockets and advertising that comes with big brand recognition.

My advice? Specialize, and be damn good at what you do. Sandwiches? You're up against the Jimmy Johns and Panera Breads of the world. Mexican, Italian, or Chinese? Be ready for some tough mom-and-pops who actually *are* Mexican, Italian, or Chinese. If you want to do BBQ or soul food but don't have it together, you will know quickly, as this is a very discerning group. Don't let any of this deter you. With a good product and—most importantly—great service, you can successfully complete with anyone out there.

You'll need to find a convenient location to work from. Look for something that already has a commercial kitchen in place, including three-bay sinks, grease traps, mop sinks, exhaust hoods, and all the related plumbing and electrical. This will save you a *ton* of money. (We'll talk more about equipment later.) You won't be serving guests inside, so don't worry about finding a space with a dining area. All you need is a kitchen and a bathroom. Along those lines, don't fixate on finding a "cute" space. No one will see it anyway. (Make your restaurant cute when you get one.) Catering doesn't require flash, so save as much as you can on upfront costs.

With regard to location, look for a space that's centrally located. That way, no delivery is too far. And don't overlook run-down or failed areas. The rents on these spaces are ridiculously low, even when they're just a couple of miles from the "high rent" district. There's usually plenty of parking, too, which makes it easier for your delivery people to get in and out. Of course, you shouldn't go into an area where you feel unsafe, but do be open-minded. If you're only doing breakfast and lunch, you'll mainly be working days anyway. Plus, you won't have any walk-in business or keep much cash in the place. As a result, you can be a little more adventurous with where you operate.

With catering, you can grow as big as you want to. You just have to hit the pavement and hustle for business.

TIPS FOR RUNNING YOUR CATERING BUSINESS

- Have a more interesting name, logo, or catchphrase than anybody else.

- Answer your phone with a live body.

- Make it easy for people to order from you. Encourage them to use a calendar you provide to order for the entire month or quarter.

- Take time to probe so you can tailor the order. Is the client a construction firm with big eaters? Send a little extra. Are you feeding a group of mostly women at a fundraising meeting? Send a little less than usual so there's no waste. Allergies? Modify some selections.

- Suggest ways to save a customer money. You'll have that customer for life.

- Be a little early with deliveries. Nobody complains when food arrives early, but God help you if you're five minutes late. That's what people will remember about your company!

Chapter 3: Choosing Your Business Model

> - Offer impeccable service. If you act like you give a damn, people will notice, and will give you jobs and precious referrals.
> - Leave plenty of cards and menus behind when you make a delivery. This leads to weekend jobs for anniversaries, bar mitzvahs, first communions, viewing parties, and the like.
> - Send holiday cards to your corporate clients and birthday cards to the salespeople and office managers who order from you.
> - As your catering business grows, contract with a restaurant delivery company. That way, you don't have to hire more drivers or lease more vehicles.

Concessions

There are some people out there who make hundreds of thousands of dollars a year as concessionaires—that is, by operating a food tent or trailer at state fairs, music festivals, bike weeks, and anywhere else folks gather outdoors. For the pros, making $80,000 cash in two weeks is not uncommon.

Some are full time, roaming from event to event all over the region or even the country. If you go this route, you may find yourself living on the road for months at a time—but the road is where the money is.

Others prefer to stay local. Rather than travelling, they stick to events in their hometown. Although staying local may not generate enough income to make your concession stand a full-time option, it's a great way to generate extra income. And, if you run it as a complement to another food business such as a catering business or a restaurant—something I'd advise rather than attempting the full-time route—it can help increase brand awareness.

Erin and I did local concessions in tandem with our catering business for about three years, and had a terrific time. We hung a banner on one side of the tent with our catering company's name and phone number, and strung the whole thing with Christmas lights. Our main hustle was the Indy Jazz Fest, where it wasn't unusual to make up to $5,000 a day selling gyros, falafels, and salads. We used two three-foot griddles—a red-hot one to sear the pre-sliced and pre-cooked gyro meat and a cooler one to keep the foldable pita bread warm and puffy. For shits and giggles, I'd pour a cup of water on the hot griddle every so often for extra sizzle, pop, and steam.

For our operation, we needed nine people in all, including Erin and me—two grill men, two finishers, three money takers, one runner, and one expediter. The runner and expediter rotated out to give people breaks. The grill men would load up the pita with meat, place it in on a paper food tray, which contained a handful of pretzels, and pass it behind them to the finishers. The finishers, who were stationed at a sandwich prep table, added lettuce, tomatoes, and tzatziki sauce. They in turn passed the tray to the money takers, who, after taking the money, handed the tray—as well as any necessary bottled beverages, which were iced down in barrels—off to the customer. From order to delivery, it took maybe 30 seconds. It's all about speed with concessions.

Over the course of time, we naturally got to know some of the other concessionaires, many of whom were full-timers. One standout was Larry. Larry was a short, stocky fellow who always wore a tank top and seemed to be perpetually sweating. I'd say he was in his early thirties. His menu of chicken wings, fries, and Italian sausages stayed the same every year. Larry worked with his wife, who was from the Dominican Republic. On weekdays, they operated several hot dog carts around town, each of which he said made $500 per day. On the weekends, they worked any and all concession opportunities, hiring a temporary staff and paying everyone in cash. They kept up this routine from April through October. After the last event in the fall, Larry and his wife would pack up and head for the Dominican Republic, where they owned property and enjoyed the sun and beaches. Come springtime, they'd come back to Indiana and do it all over again. Not a bad life. Hustle for half a year in the states and then spend winters in the Caribbean.

Whether you work concessions part time or full time, there are some major advantages to this business model:

- You don't need to lease a commercial kitchen (although you may be required to provide proof of access to an offsite commissary). Instead, you'll cook under a tent or in your own food trailer.
- You don't need to order inventory other than what you're selling at your event. Often, that will be delivered to you or held in refrigerated trucks by the vendors.
- Concessions are an all-cash business. There's no need for a point-of-sale (POS) system, and you never have to deal with Internet or software crashes.
- Labor is temporary and is hired on the spot. The pros simply take out ads for help in whatever town they'll be visiting a week or so ahead of the event.

Chapter 3: Choosing Your Business Model

- Food items are familiar, simple and straightforward, easy to prep, easy to cook, and can be purchased anywhere.
- You can start a concession business with a modest investment in equipment (which you will have to transport and store) or in a food truck or concession trailer.
- You can work as much or as little as you want.

Of course, there are some disadvantages:

- If you're full-time, it's a grind. You need to be mobile to follow the money.
- It's a gamble. Low attendance due to bad weather or poor promotion can wipe out a huge portion of your profits.
- Depending on where you live, the business may be a seasonal.

Dollar for dollar, concessions is probably the least expensive option, at least initially. You can be all in for a few thousand bucks or less. It'll take some hustle to recoup your investment, but you're not tied up in a long-term lease or responsible for regular employee wages. This fast-paced, all-cash business does require stamina and optimism.

TIPS FOR RUNNING YOUR CONCESSION STAND

- If you aren't taking the money, stand next to the people who are.

- Most people at the event will be carrying $20 bills because they stopped at an ATM on their way. Craft your menu so the ticket total adds up to $10, $15, or $20 and arrive with enough change to cover those transactions.

- If you're selling drinks, don't ask the customer "Would you like a drink?" Instead, say "And what to drink?" after they order. That way, you make the decision for them that yes, they want a drink. You will sell one the majority of the time.

- Keep things moving. If people are faced with a long line that appears to be at a standstill, they'll bypass you and go elsewhere.

- If you're at a high-volume event, have as many people taking money as you can *across* your frontage. For example, if your tent is 10 feet wide and 20 feet deep, you can comfortably fit three or even four money takers. This results in shorter lines and allows you to move more people through faster.

> - Be friendly. Smile.
> - Choose concession food that's easy to make and clean up—something people can eat easily with their hands that's not too saucy or greasy.
> - Get—and stay—plugged in to the good money-making events in your area.

Food Trucks

Food trucks are popular, and they're here to stay. They offer the flexibility of a concession stand with the brand recognition and daily availability of a brick-and-mortar restaurant. I've never operated a food truck, but Erin and I were concessionaires for a few years, and the hustle is the same. Essentially, a food truck is a concession tent on wheels.

As I see it the food-truck model offers several advantages, including the following:

- Mobility. You're not tied down to any location for any length of time on any given day.
- There's a reasonably low cost to entry. All you need is a truck. You can purchase one already outfitted or one you build out yourself.
- Minimal staffing. Often, you can get away with running the truck with three people or less.
- You can accept cash or credit cards, just like a restaurant or caterer.
- There's no rent.
- You can work as much or as little as you like.

There are also a few disadvantages:

- You'll need access to an approved commercial kitchen or commissary for prep work, which you'll need to lease at terms that make the math work for your operation.
- The weather can be your enemy. Wet days, brutal winters, and scorching summer temperatures can keep food truck patrons—who are, of course, outdoors—at bay.
- In certain markets a truck may not produce enough income to make a full-time go of it. You may need multiple trucks or live in a city where the weather and population can support your truck and everybody else's. In some cases there may simply not be enough "bodies" for everyone to share.

Chapter 3: Choosing Your Business Model

A food truck is a viable option, and definitely worth your consideration. Indeed, there are several successful food trucks operating in my city. That being said, there are also many food trucks that "used to" operate in my city. But, if things don't work out, you have an easy exit strategy: Just sell the truck. You'll definitely get out in better shape than a caterer or restaurant owner would.

> **TIP**
> Because I've never owned a food truck myself, I'm probably not the best person to advise you on starting one. I suggest you check out sources other than this book for information about the intricacies of the food-truck business.

Opening a Restaurant

We are now left with the most expensive route into foodservice: opening a full-fledged restaurant. This business model has the most potential for a dizzying return on your investment—or for a complete loss and a bunch of debt thrown in for good measure.

Most people go for opening a restaurant right away. That's understandable. It is so rewarding to have your own little corner of the world making you proud. Unfortunately, this is the riskiest option, requiring the involvement of several people and lots of money just to get going. Often, the financial outlay is astronomical—before even a single plate is sold. And your hours of operation must be competitive, meaning you very well may need to be open seven days a week

Specifically, a full-blown brick-and-mortar restaurant requires a physical space with its related lease or mortgage payments, dining-room furniture, and kitchen equipment. Odds are you'll also need cash for construction or remodeling. In addition to that, you'll have to hire dependable full-time cooks, cashiers, servers, and maybe bartenders right out of the gate.

Of course, it's possible to go the direct route and open a restaurant straightaway. But if you're looking to get into the foodservice business on the cheap, I'd proceed with extreme caution. Running a catering and concession business before opening a quick-service restaurant seemed to be the progression that worked out best for us. I often wonder if we would have survived had we opened the restaurant first. I want to believe that with drive and determination we would have, but there was so much we didn't know. My guess is that *getting* open might not have been too difficult, but *staying* open probably would have.

> **TIP**
> If I were a new food entrepreneur starting out, I'd stick with catering or some type of concession stand—mobile or stationary—because of their low barrier to entry, limited financial exposure, and minimal labor expense.

For the most part, this book focuses on running a restaurant operation—one that's open every day, with hired help—because that's what we see the most and where people seem to lose the most. Everything said about this type of operation can be applied to other models where you serve the public, so get in where you fit in. The goal is to save you time and hopefully help you make money. We can't predict how well you will do. That's up to you. But whatever you do, you must give it your best shot.

Private Chef

Before we move on, there's another option I didn't mention earlier, but that's worth discussing: personal chef. I've never been one, but I can relay what people who are have told me.

Being a personal chef gives you the independence of running your own business (you, the chef, *are* the business) without the expense and risk of opening a restaurant or catering operation. The money is good and you don't deal with employees or fixed costs. All you have to worry about is catering to a handful of wealthy clients. Plus, depending on who you meet and how you network in this category, you may enjoy some interesting perks from time to time.

One afternoon, a friend of mine who worked as a private chef called me. Like me, Eric was a medical sales refugee who eventually landed in food. He started out with a catering business, then owned and operated a breakfast and lunch bistro, and later became a private chef for a professional athlete. The last time I'd talked to him, he'd said he loved his job but was bored to death—if you can call an $80,000-a-year salary, a company car, and only working about two weeks out of the month boring. I understood where he was coming from, though. The same routine over and over probably got old. Besides, sometimes you crave action and being around people.

The reason he called was to ask if I was interested in filling in for him on a gig. For whatever reason, he couldn't take the job. The gist of it was his employer, the pro athlete, and four other players were going out of town for a little R and R. The five of them were piling into a private jet along with 15 "model/actresses" and flying to a private island in the Caribbean for a few days of fun and frolic. He mentioned a few of

Chapter 3: Choosing Your Business Model

the attendees, how everybody was cool and down to earth, and how rich people just do shit like that. They wanted to take a chef along because, well, "somebody's gotta cook." (I couldn't get past the whole "15 'model/actresses'" thing. I thought, 15?! The math says that's three *each*! Those greedy motherfuckers!) I told him I appreciated him thinking of me, but I was busy and couldn't take the job either. He said he understood, adding, "I just wanted to give you first dibs." How kind.

So how did Eric get plugged in with that crowd? It was purely by accident. One night, he was catering a party in his hometown of Atlanta that happened to be in the same condo building where a popular female R&B singer was living. She smelled his cooking in the hallway and came over to investigate. He wound up doing some work for her and, after a while, just fell into this network of celebrities and pro athletes. They became his clients and kept him in comfy, high-paying jobs. According to him, they weren't hard to work for—as long as you were discreet, dependable, and knew how to cook. I mean *for real* cook, like a southern grandmother.

With most of his clients, how it usually went down was a contract would be drawn up for a set term. They'd agree on scheduled cooking days at the client's residence along with any dietary goals or nutritional needs. Then he'd take an inventory of their kitchen and request any equipment he needed they didn't already own, which they would purchase and keep. Any special parties or catering events would be separate deals. In the case of his current job, with the pro athlete, he relocated to the city the athlete played for, found an apartment not too far from where the guy lived, and was provided a car for getting groceries and general personal use. It was easy, he said. And once he got plugged in, there was more work out there than he could handle. Sure, there were some personalities to deal with, but they were mostly normal people who loved good food and happened to be wealthy enough to pay someone to cook it for them. And they didn't mind paying top dollar for it, either.

All this is to say if you cook and you want to work for yourself, make money, and meet people who can possibly invest in your eventual restaurant or bar, being a private chef to the rich and famous is worth considering. This may be an attractive option for some of you folks coming out of culinary school, too.

Chapter 4

A Sample Business Plan

Before you go borrowing money or spending your own, you should have a clear idea of what you want to achieve. In other words, you need a business plan.

This is the time to critically dissect your concept and its expectations. There are really no shortcuts here. Doing as much upfront analysis as possible will help you be better prepared when it's time to pull the trigger. Yes, it's not as fun as shopping for equipment or building out your kitchen, but taking the time to write everything down, crunch the numbers, re-evaluate, and change where necessary will help you prove to yourself and to others that you're taking this venture seriously.

Most business plans follow a standard template, and there are many resources out there for you to peruse and adapt to your concept. In this chapter, you'll see one for an imaginary concept called Sally's Sandwiches.

> **NOTE**
> You may be tempted to skip over this chapter, but bear with me. It will help you when it comes time to build your own business plan—something I strongly urge you to do, even if all you want to do is open a snow-cone stand. Nothing beats having an analysis of your idea written down in black and white. And I promise: You'll be surprised to learn more about what you thought you already knew.

What's in a Business Plan?

A business plan covers several key areas. These include the following:

- Executive summary
- Mission and strategy
- Market
- Pricing, profitability, and break-even
- Operations
- Management and staffing
- Contingency plans
- Financial projections
- Repayment of debt

The Executive Summary

The executive summary provides an overview of the market, the proposed business and location, your management team, the loan request, and any collateral you may have. With regard to the loan request, state the amount you'll need plus a little more. You can always go down on your number if necessary, and you can always present your plan to more than one person. Also, be sure to include any supporting market research you find to show you've done your homework.

Mission and Strategy

Here's where you go into more detail as to why you want to open your business. Be sure to include your research and supporting rationale, and to show you have goals.

Market

This section should include background info, customer need and target customer, a product description, an analysis of the competition, business categories now and in the future, and plans for advertising.

Pricing, Profitability, and Break-Even

This is the area on which you and any investors you drum up need to focus. It's what people really want hear about: your numbers. This section discusses your restaurant's pricing, markup, and profit margin, and an analysis of your break-even point.

For the pricing section, you'll attach a draft of your menu with proposed pricing. Naturally, the price of each menu item will depend on the cost to the business as well as how labor intensive the item may be.

Chapter 4: A Sample Business Plan

> **NOTE**
>
> Many operators assume that in the beginning, or even after they've been at it a while, the best way to grab people's attention is to compete on price. Prices, they think, will capture the public's attention the quickest, and therefore lead to more bodies in the door. This is false. You should never chase business with low prices. Yes, you might wind up with a busy dining room, but all you'll get in return is an overworked staff and margins that won't work for you in the long run. And when you realize your error, you'll be forced to raise your prices anyway. Instead, do your research up front, and open with the highest price point you can stand.

To show your markup and profit margin, offer a snapshot of what you'll be offering. (In the sample business plan that follows, a "combo meal" was used.) How much will it cost to produce the item? How much will you sell it for? When you have these numbers, you'll be able to identify your food cost and gross margin, both of which are expressed as a percentage. A general rule is a 300% to 400% markup but it can go much higher.

> **TIP**
>
> Many food vendors have computer programs to help you cost out your menu items. This is a free service, and they want your business, so you might as well put them to work. You may even want to have this done by a few different vendors to see how you come out.

As for the break-even analysis, it reveals how many sales you need to break even. For simplicity's sake, add up your estimated *fixed costs*—rent, utilities, insurance, labor, etc.—and divide them by your gross margin. As with your food costs, you may not have hard numbers on your fixed costs just yet. That's OK. Just give these numbers your best guess, and err on the high side. In our example we are going for a $10 target sale.

> **NOTE**
>
> In addition to fixed costs, there will also be other costs, such as repairs and maintenance, professional fees, credit card–processing fees, etc. We are using the minimal numbers to keep the doors open in this example.

Operations

In this part of the business plan, you can indicate which suppliers your restaurant will use, noting names, their standing in the industry, and their payment terms.

Management and Staffing

Here, you'll indicate how many full-time and part-time employees you plan to have. You can also provide an estimate of your labor expense.

Contingency Plans

This section details how you'll deal with an unexpected downturn in sales or a slower-than-expected launch. For example, you might reduce the number of staff or the number of days or hours the business is open to decrease labor costs.

Financial Projections

The data in this section is a shot in the dark. Nevertheless, you need to include *something* here. The sample business plan that follows assumes an average 10% growth per month after an initial bump post-launch at the height of spring and a slight pullback during the vacation months of July and August. January and February are generally the slowest months. They suck for everybody in the food business.

> **NOTE**
>
> You will rarely be in the black at launch or even several months past. That's to be expected. Still, you must think positively and always bet on yourself to win. If you keep your fixed costs down, do the right things at launch, give the best service possible, and have an owner (you) who is both present and participating, you'll have a good shot at starting off with decent numbers.

Repayment of Debt

This is where you reassure your potential investor you have a plan for repayment.

Chapter 4: A Sample Business Plan

A Sample Business Plan

Sally's Sandwiches...And Soups!

Business Plan

Presented To: Folks with money to lend

By: Sally O. Smith

Executive Summary

There is a market opportunity in the better deli sandwich category in Hamilton County, Indiana generally and the city of Fishers specifically. The sandwich is without argument the quintessential American food item. The market has and continues to generate billions of dollars in sales, global acceptance, customer loyalty, and avid menu participation by restaurateurs.

The category of the better deli sandwich is one that, while maturing, shows to be the future of the segment. Consumers are demanding better quality, fresher ingredients, and local/organic produce and proteins, and they are willing to pay for them. The frequency of consumers dining out and selecting healthy sandwiches and soups is evidenced. (See attached chart.)

Proposed Business

Sally's Sandwiches proposes to fill the niche in the downtown Fishers area and its environs. It will be recognized as a locally owned destination restaurant where guests can not only get healthy sandwich meals but also a variety of other items such as soups, salads, and desserts, all made from scratch. Certain items offered can be served hot, right off a state-of-the-art panini press. The overall experience of the guest in the restaurant—from the sight-line kitchen to the music and décor, along with a superior mix of the most current foodservice technology and attentive personal service—will differentiate Sally's from its competitors.

Location

The identified location for Sally's Sandwiches is downtown Fishers, Indiana, a rapidly growing suburb north of Indianapolis. The following is demographic data supplied by ABC Commercial Real Estate Company, a local broker:

Demographics	1 Mile	3 Mile
Population	8,977	64,473
Households	3,553	24,140
Average HH Income	$111,254	$127,638

Management

Sally's will be owned and managed by Sally Smith along with industry experienced managerial staff. Sally Smith has an extensive background in customer service in the retail, insurance, and healthcare industries. With more than 15 years of experience in these fields and proven effectiveness in management, budgeting, and team leadership, she will be an on-site owner along with trained, experienced staff hired at competitive wages.

Loan Request

Sally's Sandwiches is seeking financing of $100,000. This will cover the buildout or modification of an existing space, equipment, and general operating expenses for six months. Sally's Sandwiches has cash investments of $20,000 on deposit with First Bank and Trust earmarked for the business.

Collateral

The loan will be collateralized by personal equity of real estate owned, cash on deposit, 401k savings, and the credit strength of the borrower.

Mission and Strategy

Sally's Sandwiches plans to be the premiere lunch and dinner destination for healthy fare. It will provide unusual and exciting menu choices, be competitively priced, be expertly prepared, and be delivered to the customer with the utmost in professional service and courtesy—while still maintaining the convenience

Chapter 4: A Sample Business Plan

and accessibility of a quick-service restaurant. Upon the successful launch of the business model, Sally's will open opportunities in surrounding counties and states for franchisees to bring the experience and flavor of its concept to its communities.

Market

Background

There are several sandwich shop players currently operating in the Fishers area. Some are in the "better" category, while others offer a quick, budget-friendly dining option—albeit not as high quality. When assessing this category the differentiation of Sally's from these players could include the following:

- A premium protein offering, sourced and delivered locally
- Premium cheeses
- All items sliced, chopped, or grilled in-store
- A premium bun or roll from local bakeries
- Handcrafted condiments made in-store
- Fresh soups made daily
- Unique and original creations, to include world influences
- Premium pricing

The Customer Need and the Target Customer

The Sally's Sandwiches customer is an individual who looks to spend $10 or more on lunch or dinner for fresh, made-to-order meals, but doesn't have time to sit down at a full-service restaurant and deal with all that entails (servers, gratuity, etc.). Sally's will be family friendly and offer hand-dipped milkshakes and fruit smoothies. At present, there are no plans to serve alcohol.
Point-of-sale items will include bottled waters, low-carb/low-cal fruit waters, gourmet kettle-cooked potato chips, and the like. Research continues to support the notion that consumers are demanding healthy choices when they're on the go, so in addition to our premium deli meats, Sally's will offer grilled boneless and skinless chicken breasts and a grilled fish option. There will be a rotating selection of vegetarian-friendly choices. Dessert items will include homemade double chocolate chunk cookies, blonde brownies, and a "pie o' the week."

Restaurant Winners

The market for those who enjoy the traditional soup and sandwich but are tired of choices that offer little taste, haphazard assembly, or dubious ingredients is the niche that Sally's intends to fill. Consumers are upgrading their palates, and want new and different options.

Product Description

Sally's intends to source as many ingredients from local farmers (in season), butcher shops, and bread makers as possible. This ensures freshness and accountability with the supply chain and strengthens local economies. Meals will be prepared in full view of the customer to maintain the level of trust and confidence we share with our guests. Gluten-free bread will be available, and naturally, we'll be able to address any allergen concerns.

Competitive Analysis and Advantage

Let's examine some competition in the greater Fishers and Indianapolis area on either end of the sandwich or deli-style restaurant spectrum.

Business	Avg. Guest Check ($)	Quality/Presentation
Panera Bread	$12	Good/Very Good
Subway	$7	Average/Good
McAllister's	$12	Good/Very Good

Our personal analysis based on comparative dining experiences indicates Sally's should be a worthy competitor with these restaurants, most of whom have thrived in this segment for decades. Our edge:

- We will offer premium, locally sourced products.
- Our rotating "taste of the world" choices will be unusual and bold.
- Our décor will reflect the tastes and interests of the local population.
- We will have a totally open prep and service kitchen.
- Our guest check will average between $10 and $13.

Sally's intends to operate in a smaller footprint than most of its competition (approximately 1,300 to 1,800 square feet). Lower overhead means bigger reinvestment in quality ingredients and staff.

Chapter 4: A Sample Business Plan

Business Categories Now and in the Future

Sally's Sandwiches will primarily operate in the fast-casual or quick-service arena. The guest will order at a counter and pay first. The order will then be called out for pickup or delivered to the guest's seat. This gives the guest the convenience and speed of fast food but the attentiveness of casual dining. As the brand grows, we'll explore all niches for our product, which may include a catering arm as well as a breakfast menu. Interest in the culture, brand, and unique menu items may sprout the addition of retail items such as apparel, mugs and glassware, and a boutique line of custom sauces, condiments, and beverages.

Advertising

The budget for advertising will focus on pre-launch and grand-opening activities to market Sally's, included but not limited to radio, TV, flyers, website, and billboards. Press releases to local media and invitations to special previews for local food and lifestyle writers are planned, as well as menu distributions and owner introductions throughout a three-mile radius to businesses, churches, schools, clubs, and offices. Social media accounts on Facebook, Twitter, and Instagram have been established and will go live at appropriate time.

Pricing, Profitability, and Break-Even

Pricing

Our proposed menu, with prices, is attached.

Markup and Profit Margin

Sally's will market a combo meal as the guest's best bet for a balanced meal, ease of ordering, and best value. The combo meal will include a sandwich, cup of soup, and beverage.

The cost breakdown of the combo meal is as follows:

Restaurant Winners

Ingredient	Cost
4 oz roasted turkey breast	$1.24
Artisan bread (2 slices)	$0.27
Cheese (1 slice)	$0.25
Lettuce	$0.01
Tomato	$0.01
Red onion	$0.01
Craft mayo (1 Tbsp)	$0.03
Homemade soup of the day (8 oz cup)	$0.45
Handcrafted flavored lemonade or tea (16 oz)	$0.20

The estimated costs to Sally's for its signature combo meal offering would be $2.47, and will be offered at retail for $9.99 (before tax).

Food cost: $2.47/$9.99 = 24.7%

Gross margin: 75.3% (0.247 − 1 = 0.7527)

Projected Break-Even Analysis

Fixed costs (monthly) are estimated as follows:

Item	Cost
Rent (triple net)	$3,000
Electric	$1,000
Gas	$800
Business insurance	$250
Workman's comp insurance	$200
Phone/cable/Internet	$250
Salaries	$14,060
Total	$19,560/month

Chapter 4: A Sample Business Plan

Break-even volume (sales per month needed to break even): $19,560/.753 = $25,976

Operations

Suppliers

Sally's Sandwiches and Soups will primarily use the following vendors:

- Pete's Produce
- ABC Foodservice
- Betty the Bread Lady
- Mike's Mighty Meat

All are reputable and have good standing and tenure in the marketplace. Most accounts are payable with 7 to 21 day net terms with the option of COD at our preference.

Management and Staffing

Sally's intends to operate with an initial staff of four full-time employees (owner included) and anywhere between four and six part-time employees. Sally will oversee kitchen operations along with a kitchen manager. Front of house will be led by designated shift leaders working in conjunction with the owner.

Employees

Full- and part-time employees experienced in foodservice will be hired at a competitive wage and will be trained by ownership.

Salary Expenses

Total monthly compensation can vary seasonally, but is estimated as follows (assuming business hours of Monday through Sunday, 11 a.m. to 9 p.m.):

Employee	Compensation
Kitchen manager (salaried)	$2,500
Cooks and cashiers	$11,560

To calculate the total monthly compensation for cooks and cashiers, it's assumed there will be two front-of-house (FOH) and two back-of-house (BOH) employees (not including kitchen manager and owner) Monday through Thursday and three FOH and three BOH employees (not including kitchen manager and owner) Friday through Sunday, averaging $8.50/hour.

Monday through Thursday labor estimate: $1,360/week

Friday through Sunday labor estimate: $1,530/week

FOH/BOH total labor estimate: $2,890/week or $11,560/month

Contingency Plans

In the event of an unexpected downturn in sales or a slower-than-expected launch, the number of staff can be reduced by one person on weekends. In addition, we could consider being open six days per week instead of seven, reducing labor expenses by approximately $2,000/month.

Financial Projections

YEAR ONE					
March	April	May	June	July	August
$15,124	$18,730	$21,669	$26,942	$25,247	$24,996
September	October	November	December	January	February
$27,395	$30,034	$33,937	$37,330	$25,795	$24,992
YEAR TWO					
March	April	May	June	July	August
$30,419	$33,360	$36,596	$39,156	$37,555	37082
September	October	November	December	January	February
$40,377	$44,799	$49,938	$53,433	$41,001	$41,544

Repayment of Debt

Assuming break even at the 90- to 120-day mark with a successful launch, continued community outreach, advertising, and word of mouth, debt service should be easily managed.

In Closing...

Remember, this is just a template to get started. You can plug in whatever concept you're thinking about. Drilling down to the nuts and bolts of your operation is a proper first step to critically looking at what you're facing and how to plan. These are very basic numbers and designed to get you to understand the plan from a broad view. When actual numbers start coming in you can break things down six ways to Sunday.

Don't just write your business plan before you open and forget about it. It's a fluid document. If anything, it will be even more valuable after you get up and running. Make it a point to revisit it and plug in real numbers. That way, if you find yourself seeking financing from new investors or considering opening additional locations, you'll have accurate data on hand.

> **NOTE**
> Although your business plan is useful, it'll be your profit and loss statement that offers a true snapshot of your business's performance. You'll learn more about that later in this book.

Chapter 5

Getting Your Finances in Order

After a year of catering, I had burned through my 401k. Fortunately, I ran out of money just when the business got steady enough to pay its own bills, with a little something left over for me. Naturally, I was feeling pretty good as I watched business steadily increase and basked in my modest entrepreneurial success. That didn't last long, however.

For a while there, it was like I got hit with one punch after another. First, I needed a new (used) van. That cost around $7,000. Then the furnace in my fixer-upper duplex gave out—in the middle of winter—and the building we bought when we moved the business needed a new roof. At the same time, I was helping my mother, who had made some major financial missteps, which nearly cost her her home. And of course, the taxman was due his piece from the 401k cash-out. I swear, every cent of profit that came in went back out to something else.

You'll need enough cash to weather storms like these. That means ensuring your personal finances are in order, as well as making sure you have enough money when you start the business to see it through. No matter the concept, if you remain ignorant to how the numbers need to work, the discussions, plans, and ideas are, as Sidney Poitier said in *A Piece of the Action*, "masturbation." That is, it may make you feel good, but it does not produce life.

Cleaning Up Your Own House

Before you even start to think about scraping the money together to launch your food business, you must assess your current financial situation from a personal perspective. If you have extensive credit-card debt or a car or house that needs major repairs, I strongly suggest handling that as best you can before you make plans to open *anything*. Along these same lines, if you have an expensive gambling or drug habit, now would be the time to cut back or walk away. The idea is to start from the strongest cash and credit position you can before borrowing large sums of money or spending your own.

Financing Your Operation

Where can you get financing? That's the six-million-dollar question. You'll need capital for your concept, and that capital will have to come from you and/or someone else. Let's start with the "someone else" model.

Naturally, the first place most people turn when they want a loan is a bank. Unfortunately, in most cases, if you're opening a restaurant, you can forget about the bank. They just don't play. That leaves you one other option: begging other people for money. As far as these investors go, there are two primary types:

- **Debt investors:** Simply put, a debt investor is a person who'll loan you money at specified terms. You pay the person back, with interest, and you each go your own way after the debt is satisfied. This is probably the most common and easiest route in the beginning.
- **Equity investors:** An equity investor becomes a part owner and shares in the profits while you, the operator, do the work. In return for a piece of the business, this person takes the ride right alongside you, through thick and thin, good times and bad. He or she may hang around for the long haul. Alternatively, at some point, you might buy him or her out.

Both types of investors have their advantages and disadvantages, and you can be as creative as you wish structuring these deals. You'll want to make sure you establish agreements with regard to compensation, sweat equity, and rates of return, as well as how much power they have over your operation. There should also be an exit strategy that is amenable to everyone. And of course, everything should be in writing.

> **NOTE**
>
> No matter how well your place does, you really can't "win" if you never pay back your debt. All you did was play restaurateur for a little while. Margins can be very thin in this business, so the quicker you get to the plus side, the better.

For some people, friends and family members make for good investors. If you find the need to go begging to them for money, let there be no shame in your efforts. After all, they love you, they love your ambition, and they want to see you succeed. Just keep these points in mind:

Chapter 5: Getting Your Finances in Order

- Be professional.
- Present an actual business plan.
- Be serious about your plans and goals.

> **NOTE**
> If you aren't a jerk, you exhibit effort and drive, and you have protected your reputation, you shouldn't have any reservations about asking people to invest with you.

Anyone with half a brain knows foodservice is the riskiest game in town. So be prepared for a thorough scrubbing of your business plan, and don't take rejections personally. Your biggest hurdle will be your lack of experience. If someone takes a pass, ask what weaknesses in your idea led to that decision and work on strengthening them. You need to examine your concept and goals with complete objectivity. You can always walk away and come back with a refined plan.

If you do find an investor, that person will likely expect you to have at least *some* skin in the game. That means coming up with some of the money yourself. Or, you may find yourself unable to secure any investors at all, in which case you'll need to come up with *all* of the money yourself. This may involve liquidating savings accounts, mortgaging real estate, or tapping into retirement plans. This is risky—not to mention scary. It's your money, and once it's gone, it's gone. The upside of flying solo, without an investor, is that you're the boss. You answer to no one but yourself, and you don't owe anybody anything. For better or worse, everything is resting on your shoulders.

How Much Do You Need?

This one's easy: Double what you think.

A good starting point is to estimate how much you need to open your restaurant and survive personally and professionally for a period of one year. Now, I know that sounds like a lot of money, and it is. But remember: The barrier to entry for restaurants is higher than for other areas of foodservice because there are so many moving parts.

Expect to overspend your first time out. You'll find that if you can stick around, things will get cheaper after you open more locations or new concepts. You learn where the savings are, what matters (and doesn't matter) to the public, and how to be creative with spaces you come across that, while not perfect, can come in at a real bargain.

Restaurant Winners

The bottom line? The market weeds out the weakest players but richly rewards the strongest. It's this risk—this gamble—that drives many of us to go all in and see what "this thing" we have might do.

Chapter 6

Location, Location, Location

You now have a concept, a business plan, and some money lined up (most of it probably yours). Your next step is to look for a location.

Choosing an Area

Let's say you live in an average-sized city with a population of 1,000,000 people. Most likely, it can be broken down into four main areas:

- Downtown/central business district (CBD)
- Midtown
- The "downtown donut" (my term, apologies to any urban planners)
- The suburbs

> **TIP**
>
> If you can, go for the "ugly duckling" in the best location. Again, I said location, not neighborhood. You can locate in virtually any neighborhood in foodservice, catering being one example and price point for a targeted demographic being another.

Downtown/CBD

This is the core or center city, where the majority of major businesses, city hall, and other federal or state offices are found. Perhaps there's a mall or other dense retail component, as well as long-standing residential buildings mixed with new developments.

Because people are rapidly repopulating downtowns across the country, this area might be a great choice for a demographic that's young, single, and gainfully employed.

Restaurant Winners

Downtown residents love the walkable proximity of bars and restaurants. And unless they're brown-bagging it, weekday office workers provide a captive audience.

There are several advantages to opening a food business here:

- There are huge numbers of people in this area, with money to spend on dining or catering.
- You have access to a large, experienced labor pool.
- You will receive reliable service from suppliers. Downtown customers get the earliest deliveries because it makes sense for delivery drivers to navigate downtown streets and alleys before the morning rush hour.
- Because most conventions and special events are downtown, you'll get great exposure to both locals and out-of-towers.
- Thanks to the number of people who work in these areas, you'll have a captive audience on a daily basis.
- Many downtowns are now enjoying a residential boom, with new apartments and condominiums that include street-level retail.

In addition, there are several disadvantages:

- You'll face more competition from established local businesses and popular national brands.
- There may be limited dayparts. (A *daypart* is a time segment that divides the day. For example, maybe your central business district becomes a ghost down after 5 p.m. In that case, you might opt for a breakfast and/or lunch rather than a dinner concept.
- It may empty out on weekends and major holidays, when everybody's off work.
- Although experienced labor is available, employees may have trouble getting to work on time due to traffic or congestion. In addition, paying for daily parking may be unattractive.
- Downtown competitors can poach your best talent.
- Rents are high and ownership of your space may be impossible.
- Well-financed national brands generally scoop up the best locations. Moreover, they often have the wherewithal to stay open even if sales are soft. It may be a stretch to call them "loss leaders," but they can stand a downturn a lot longer than most of us, making it hard for a local independent to compete.

Chapter 6: Location, Location, Location

Midtown

This area, typically several miles from downtown, will have long-established neighborhoods with larger households. It offers the biggest residential density with the most diversity. Schools, churches, and businesses are abundant. Midtown may have several arteries that travel most of the way—if not all the way—to the CBD. These arteries likely have pockets of restaurant and retail, either free-standing or in strip malls, which may be suitable for your concept.

Opening a restaurant in midtown offers various plusses:

- You'll have a variety of spaces to choose from with respect to square footage, location, and design.
- Generally, there's an even mix of breakfast, lunch, and dinner dayparts.
- You'll have an easily accessible labor pool.
- A midtown site may offer better—or even free—parking for guests and staff.
- Rents are competitive.
- Landlords may be more willing to negotiate the terms of your lease.
- It's convenient for quick trips to grocery stores or other suppliers if you're in a jam and need product.
- Your peers will include many more mom-and-pops and independent restaurants.
- If you choose, you can be open seven days a week, 24 hours a day, and even holidays, and *still* capture business.

There are also minuses:

- You will still be up against big national brands, who will likely claim the best corners.
- While there is generally a good labor pool, experience levels may vary. Many will be part-timers and students, and turnover could be an issue.
- Business can be a little unpredictable week to week, month to month. Weather can keep people home and various construction projects or street maintenance can cause problems.
- Your deliveries may come a little later from suppliers as they work their way outward from downtown.

If you do decide to set up shop on a midtown artery, determine whether you want to be on the downtown (going into work) side or the uptown (on the way home) side. If you have a coffee shop or breakfast concept, it may fare better on the downtown side because of inbound rush-hour traffic. If your concept is a quick- or full-service restaurant, you could have stronger numbers on the uptown side. Either way, drive the area multiple times at different hours to gauge how much of a hassle it will be to get to your door.

> **TIP**
>
> Is there a place in your favorite area that's struggling? If so, wait to pounce on that property when the business closes. Even better, contact the property owner to let them know if the space becomes available soon, they have an interested party.

The "Downtown Donut"

I like to call the ring about a mile outside the CBD the "downtown donut." In many cities, these areas are trendy, newly gentrified, and on the comeback for retail and residency. Much of the real estate in this area is in the form of wonderful, free-standing structures with great architectural features.

If you decide to open in the donut, you'll have most of the same pluses and minuses as you would with a midtown location. In addition, you'll want to consider these points:

- Rent can be a bargain in the donut if you get there early enough. And unlike downtown sites, ownership of your building may be in reach.
- The donut may lack the residential density of midtown or the suburbs.
- Similar to downtown, the donut typically plays home to more singles and childless couples, meaning you and your peers will likely be competing for the same customers.
- Parking may or may not be an issue in the donut.
- If you offer lunch, and your clientele consists mainly of downtown workers, you'll have to maintain tip-top efficiency to move those folks in and out quickly. Most people have at most an hour for lunch, and that includes the time it takes to travel to and from your business. Odds are, they'll be in a rush!

The Suburbs

The suburbs lie outside the city, often (but not always) beyond the interstate belt or loop circling the city proper.

Chapter 6: Location, Location, Location

> **NOTE**
>
> There are new suburbs and old suburbs. Old suburbs are those areas that were newer suburbs 30 years ago. They have the characteristics of a traditional suburb (parking, strip malls, an auto-centric layout), but are aging and in disrepair. I consider new suburbs ones that push out into entirely different counties. These suburbs have poached many of the businesses and residents who used to live in the old suburbs. Although old suburbs may no longer be pretty to look at, they house a vast sea of population (albeit with lower incomes in some cases). That may make them an attractive location for your business.

Setting up shop in the suburbs offers several key benefits:

- There are newer retail spaces with plenty of free parking (usually in a strip-mall setting).
- The demographic in newer suburbs generally consists of homeowners, families, and people with a higher income.
- Rents can be competitive, but may be higher depending on the development's demographic targets and its anchor tenants.
- Your concept can perform reasonably well with most dayparts.
- With respect to crime, they can be a safer place to operate.
- It may be easier to obtain a space that was previously occupied by another restaurant. (I'll talk more about this in a moment.)

Here are the drawbacks:

- There may be fewer free-standing buildings for lease or purchase—and those available may be priced outside your comfort zone.
- Finding labor can be challenging. If you're in a high income area, you may have a labor shortage simply because people there don't want or need to work foodservice jobs. Or it might be because when you're in the 'burbs, your labor from the city has to travel farther to get to work—something many might prefer not to do.
- If you locate in a bedroom community, your daytime sales may be softer than your city counterparts. If everybody goes into town for work, there may be fewer people left behind to support your breakfast or lunch dayparts.
- Landlords may be less flexible and command higher rents because they can.

- Many people find the suburbs boring places to work or visit.
- You may have to spend more on advertising and promotions to compete with chains that flood the suburbs.

> **TIP**
>
> As you look for a location, consider where *you* live. If you can swing it, it's not a bad idea to open your business close to home. Think about it: If you live in the suburbs but your business is downtown (or vice versa), running back home to grab something you forgot while fighting rush hour traffic or making other impromptu trips at odd hours will get old real quick—not to mention the fuel expense and wear and tear on your vehicle. We've been lucky enough to never live more than 15 minutes away from our businesses, and it's definitely come in handy!

Assessing the Location

Suppose you've found a space for your concept. How can you tell if it's right for you?

As a first step, stand outside and drink in the area. Take a critical look at what's around it—the streets, driveways, and alleyways. How's the traffic flow? What kind of delivery trucks come and go, and at what times? Where do people park? Are there any shared or common spaces?

The reason I'm telling you do this is not because I want you to gauge whether you'll get enough business. In fact, I *never* want you to think about whether enough people will walk through your doors. Rather, I want you to imagine having *too much* business. As you're standing there, ask yourself, what if 100 people come here at once? How would it flow? Can everybody get in and out? In other words, what's the plan for when it's so damn busy, you can't see straight?

> **TIP**
>
> Give yourself time to do recon on your prospective location. See how things look on different days of the week and, if possible, in different seasons. How much foot and vehicle traffic is there on a Sunday? How busy is it during the winter?

Chapter 6: Location, Location, Location

Now let's talk about what's inside. If you're working with very little money—or even if you're not—I strongly recommend you find a space that has previously held (or currently holds) a restaurant. In fact, I'd go so far as to eliminate any space that does not meet this criterion. Why? Because that way, you won't have to build out a kitchen from scratch, saving thousands of dollars and months of time. Yes, limiting your search in this way can be very difficult in certain markets and areas. For example, finding an existing restaurant space in the donut can be tricky. Still, you should build out a kitchen only as a last resort.

> **NOTE**
>
> Chances are, that quaint historic house or small building you want to convert to a restaurant comes with countless zoning headaches, structural issues, and remonstrators. Truth be told, it's not worth going through all that—unless you're buying structure. Otherwise, if you make that investment in a space you don't own and it fails, the only one who benefits is the landlord—and the next person who leases the space.

If the space is within in city limits, it's probably worth a trip downtown to see about any future construction projects headed to your area in the next few years. If there's a bridge repair, highway project, or other major plan to close roads or divert traffic for a lengthy period of time, you may want to reconsider that location. Also, make sure the space is not situated near city or utility property. Otherwise, you may have a different issue altogether. I know an operator, who, after obtaining variances from the city for sidewalk fencing and seating, discovered a portion of said area encroached on a utility easement. The utility informed him if he wished to use that small section of land, he'd have to pay a monthly fee. Non-negotiable, of course.

> **NOTE**
>
> Every so often, you'll come across a location or space, and a whole new concept will reveal itself to you. It may be a total 180 from your original idea! Maybe that corner is screaming for a breakfast joint, not the sandwich shop you had envisioned. Or maybe that hole in the wall would work better for banging out tacos than as a coffee shop. Be on the lookout for these types of places, and be open to changing up your idea if need be.

Should You Buy or Lease?

If you're lucky enough to find a diamond in the rough, and the price and location work for your concept, by all means buy the property if you can. You'll be the one putting the blood, sweat, and tears (not to mention money) into the demo, buildout, and furnishing of the building. If things don't work out but you own the building, you can always try a new concept or lease it out to someone else who thinks he can make it work.

If it's not possible for you to buy the building, that's OK. Most people can't. In fact, some of the most venerable restaurants in my city have been in leases 20 or 30 years. Just remember: If you don't own the space, you have to play by the landlord's rules.

A commercial lease is a contract, and it's crucial that you have a thorough understanding of its terms. That way, if the roof starts leaking in your dining room, you'll know who's responsible. And if the landlord wants a three-year personal guarantee, you'll know what to say. To that end, it's a good idea to have a professional commercial real estate broker represent you before making this significant financial commitment. A flawed or overly expensive lease will bring about your restaurant's demise faster than you can say, "Why did I get myself into this?"

Remember, too, what whatever the number might be--$3,000, $5,000, $8,000, $10,000 or more—it will be due each and every month, rain or shine, hot or cold, day or night. During January blizzards and slow muggy Julys, during flash floods in April and six-month street repairs, the rent will come due.

Whether you're negotiating to purchase a space or to lease it, don't let it slip away over something silly. Sometimes it's worth it to let the other guy win—or at least *think* he has—if it means you'll wind up with the space you really want. Case in point: When we paid the sellers the $60,000 "they had in it" for our first restaurant, we knew damn well they had spent nowhere near that amount for the equipment and improvements. But, given our financial situation, we weren't in a position to walk. The location was perfect for our concept, and if we didn't pull the trigger, we would never have opened. It's said the best deals are ones where both sides know something the other doesn't. In our case, *we* knew that as long as we didn't fuck it up, we would make the money back fairly quickly. *They* knew they were unloading a twice-failed location to two chumps who were willing to overpay for it. In the end, it was a win-win. They doubled their money and we bought a turnkey space, installed our concept, and were in the black in a little over 90 days.

Chapter 6: Location, Location, Location

> **NOTE**
>
> Clearly, there is such a thing as a bad deal. You don't want to concede too much by being too hasty. Otherwise, you'll start in a much more stressful financial position than necessary. If you're unsure in the least, go back to your business plan and crunch the numbers. If, in the end, the decision makes sense, go for it!

Do we own or lease? For now, we lease. At the end of our lease term, we can choose to exercise an option to continue for another five years at a pre-agreed escalation. At the end of those five years, two things could happen: the landlord could kick us out or we could re-sign with new terms. If we can't agree on the terms or if the landlord has other plans for the property, for all intents and purposes, our business at that location is finished. That's just how it goes.

One Last Thing

Yes, location is important. No one is denying that. But have you ever noticed how there are some premium locations—spaces on busy blocks that offer great access—that change concepts every 24 months? And how there are other out-of-the-way, hard-to-get-to places that still pack people in after 10, 15, or even 20 years? Be flexible, don't be afraid to look at non-traditional spaces, and don't let the good ones get away.

Let's chat with a commercial broker about leases.

Interview with Jack Esselman, Commercial Real Estate Broker

How long have you been in the real estate business?

41 years.

Suppose I'm looking for space for a restaurant or catering kitchen. Prices are presented in terms of square feet. How do I figure out the rent?

Let's keep the numbers simple. If it is $20 a foot for 2,500 feet, that would be $50,000 a year. Divided by 12 that would be $4,167 a month.

What does "triple net" mean?

What triple net means is the rent that you're paying goes to your landlord without any deductions. That means that you, the tenant, are paying your share of the real estate taxes, the insurance on the building itself, and any maintenance, both exterior and interior.

Say I'm into lease negotiations and I see something about a "personal guarantee."

What you have to watch out for there is if you're married and the landlord says "I want you and your wife/husband on the lease." Then you're pretty well nailed down. When a landlord asks for a personal guarantee from someone I represent, what I negotiate—or try to negotiate—is, "OK Mr. Landlord, how much money are you putting into the deal?" In other words, are you repairing the roof? Are you giving me new HVAC? What are you doing for me? And if that number is, let's say, 10 grand, then I say to the landlord, "Instead of us signing a personal guarantee, if my rent is"—pick a number—"$2,500 then I will give you liquidated damages"—a term that's used—"of $15,000 if I default." Which means if I default, if there's an uncured default, you get 15 grand, we call it a day, and I walk away. So what you do there is pick a number and that's the number he gets if you default. He gets his 10 grand back he put into the building plus two month's rent.

Say I've signed a five-year lease and, after the second year, things aren't looking good and I have to close down. There're three years left on the lease. What happens to me?

Basically, any lease will have a tenant default clause. Those are the remedies the landlord has when you default. There are any number of ways to handle a default clause. What a sharp landlord will ask for is called the "acceleration of rent." What that means is if you're paying $15,000 a year and you default in your first year, he can say, "I'm going to accelerate rent on those remaining four years so you owe me 60 grand." Lump sum. Now, in some states, that's illegal. That's why it depends on what state you're in. As a broker representing a tenant, I always try to get rid of acceleration of rent. The landlord will fight that, because if you say, "OK, I'll pay you 'as due,'" then the landlord says, "Well, that means I have to sue you every month." So you look for something in between as a way that he'll accept it and it doesn't burden the tenant. That's why the liquidated damage clause is usually pretty nice as a way to mediate going through that hassle.

Chapter 6: Location, Location, Location

Let's say I close up shop and the landlord finds a tenant in, say, three months. Can we call it a wash? Will he leave me alone?

A landlord always has a duty to mitigate his damages. If it goes to court, the judge will say to him, "Have you tried to re-lease this space, Mr. Landlord? You have a duty to do that." So he does that. He goes out and finds somebody for the space. They say, "Well Mr. Landlord, I'll take the space. I know you were getting $10 a foot from Mark, but I'll give you $7. Oh, and by the way, I need you to fix the roof." Well now the landlord can go back to the tenant and say, "You have to make up the balance between $7 and $10. Oh, and by the way, you're on the hook for the new roof because that's the only way I'm going get the new tenant to come in to mitigate because you left me high and dry here."

Let's say I found a space that doesn't conform to what I'm trying to do and I will need a variance from the city.

You go ahead and negotiate a lease and you have a contingency. It just says, if I don't get my variance, then we don't have a deal. If I do, then we have a firm deal and we're ready to go. It's like buying a house.

My landlord's lost the property in a tax sale or bankruptcy. I have seven years left on my lease and business is fine. My lease is still safe, right?

Any lease should have a subordination and non-disturbance clause. What subordination means is if there's a mortgage on the property, if the landlord loses the property, the mortgagee—the person who owns the paper—becomes your landlord. And what non-disturbance says from the tenant's point of view is as long as you're not in default and you're honoring the lease, then if the lender takes back the property, they become your landlord, and your lease is still good. Instead of paying the landlord, you pay the mortgagee. You have to specifically have non-disturbance in your lease to get that.

So this is why I should hire a broker when shopping properties. I shouldn't do this on my own.

Yep. Probably not.

I found a space, the terms are good, and we can get a deal done. What are some of the extras I should ask for?

There is a saying in real estate, and that is, "If you name the price, I get to name the terms. If you name the terms, then I get to name the price." From a tenant's perspective, if the landlord says, "This space is worth $20 a foot," the way you negotiate is you say, "OK, I'll give you the $20. However, I need you to do this, this, and this, and I'm going to need 90 days to open for business." If the landlord says, "I want $20 a foot," and you say, "Well I'll give you $15, and I need you to do A, B, C, and D," the landlord may turn around and say, "Hey, wait a minute. I just cut my rent by 25%. You do A, B, C, and D." Again, it's a function of how good the space is, how bad you want it, and how bad the landlord wants to lease it.

If I do hire a broker, the landlord pays their commission, right?

Normally, the landlord pays the commission. But again, you should always ask that question up front. If you're dealing with what I would call a "national landlord," in the old days, those companies would never pay commissions. So that's a question you need to ask ahead of time with the broker. Then it's up to the broker to go to the landlord and say, "Who's paying my fee?" Then that just becomes a part of the negotiation.

Let's say I don't have a broker. I call a number on a sign and I'm dealing with a landlord directly—a mom and pop—and we get to the point of a lease. Should I hire a broker to review the lease?

At that point, I'd hire an attorney. Honestly, a broker can advise a tenant on the economics of a lease, but when you get into default clauses, condemnation, force majeure, subleasing, all of that arcane stuff in a lease, it's a good idea to have an attorney do that stuff.

Never represent yourself in complex matters.

Right.

What percent should my rent be of sales?

In the old days, rent for restaurants was 5% of sales. But again, a lot of that becomes a function of what the margins are. If you're selling alcohol, which has a big margin in it, you can probably pay more.

Chapter 6: Location, Location, Location

I want to buy someone out and take over their space with my concept. I'm bound to their lease, right?

Again, it's a function of the lease. If the person's business you're buying has the right to assign that lease, then they can assign that lease and its terms to you.

That has to be in there, though.

It has to be in the lease. As a practical matter, if the landlord knows his current tenant isn't making it, he wants somebody in there that's going to pay the rent. So depending on what the lease says, you either want to take that lease as it stands with its options or you renegotiate the lease. Hell, maybe that's why the guy failed—he's paying too much rent.

I'm brand new to the restaurant business and want to open a small sandwich shop. If you had a couple of bullet points for me on how *not* to get into too much trouble with a lease, what would you tell me?

If you are concerned about how viable your venture is going to be, you probably want a short-term lease with lots of options. If you can get a three-year lease with five three-year options, that's perfect. The problem with a restaurant is that most restaurants require some pretty extensive capital infusions to get started. You need to take that into account before you even get into the business. If you take a vanilla box and you have to do all the work, you're probably going to spend $40 a foot turning that into your restaurant. To me, if the tenants have this great desire to open a restaurant, I would always recommend they try to find a closed restaurant so they can take advantage of what's there.

You've seen a lot of deals over the years.

Every deal always has glitches. There's no such thing as a clean deal.

Everything is kind of a crapshoot.

Well, I represented a guy many years ago who had a waterbed business.

Early seventies (laughs)?

Yeah, yeah, yeah. And they went gangbusters and started a little chain and basically it went bad. I used to represent a Western wear company. We did our first deal in '79 we got up to 16 locations throughout the country. And well, like the owner said to me, "Everybody and anybody that wanted to own a pair of cowboy boots now owns 'em. And the thing about cowboy boots is unless you're a rancher, they don't wear out. So, we don't have any repeat business." So yeah (laughs). I think we shut it down in '99.

So he had a good run

Oh yeah, he had a great run. Great run.

Chapter 7

A Sample Timeline to Opening Day

Between the time you develop your concept and opening day, there are lots of things—both little and big—that you need to take care of. This chapter provides a countdown to opening day—a timeline of sorts. It may be longer or shorter depending on your concept. Above all, your focus should be *not rushing*.

> **CAUTION**
>
> No doubt, you are eager to get your business up and running ASAP. Maybe you're worried someone with a similar idea will beat you to the market. Or maybe you want to make sure you get into a category while it's still hot. These are legitimate concerns. But moving too hastily will almost guarantee additional stress and unnecessary overspending. Take your time. Patience will be your friend in the end.

When Should You Open?

If you live in a densely populated city on either coast or somewhere down south, you can probably open any time of year because you have a) good weather and/or b) a large enough population to get a decent push at launch. If, however, you live in the northern states or the Midwest (like I do), then early spring is the ideal time to open.

Spring is a time of new beginnings. The stress of the holiday months—November and December—is long gone, as are the ice-cold months of January and February. March can be a funky month weather-wise, so I wouldn't open earlier than that.

Apart from weather, I'm big on opening in early spring for these reasons:

- Everybody is in town. College kids, families, and the lunch crowd are in full effect. In comparison, there's a palpable void in during the summer months of July and August, as people are traveling and school is out.
- The summer music, food, and drink festivals haven't ramped up yet, drawing away precious weekend business.
- It gives you time to work out the kinks before the crowds get too heavy. If this is your first rodeo, you *will* be on a steep learning curve during the first 30 to 60 days of your opening. You'll be learning your crowd, adjusting staff, getting your ordering straight, and identifying what works and what doesn't as you settle into your groove. That's OK! But it's best to figure out what you're doing in the early spring before you cruise into early summer and fall, which tend to be busier.

Some people like fall openings. If you live in big enough city to make this work, then fine. Otherwise, I'm convinced that seasonality can be a difference-maker. Think about it: Right when you work the kinks out, you'll be facing the dead zone of winter—a period when sales are sluggish even under the *best* of circumstances. Now, you'll have to get through the coldest months of the year with higher utility bills, icy streets, and smaller crowds.

Of course, for every rule, there's the exception. A popular Chicago pizza restaurant opened here in the middle of winter and the reception was excellent—there were two-hour wait times and their online ordering was booked solid for two weeks. But this was a big-name brand with decades of history behind it. They commanded that type of opening because they've been around for years and have a solid fan base.

24–12 Months to Opening Day

If you want to open a new restaurant, 24 months seems like an eternity. But trust me: It will pass very quickly. To give yourself the best shot possible, take ample time to research and to talk with as many people relevant to what you're doing as you can.

The very first thing you should do is get yourself checked out. You need to be in decent physical and mental shape for the long hours and stress and strain that lay ahead. Keep up with any medications and make time for your normal exercise routines. If you're transitioning from a job or another entrepreneurial pursuit, take a week or so off to relax and focus on what's coming. The foodservice business is its own unique animal and will require clear thought and as calm a mind as you can muster. Go meditate on a mountaintop, relax in a quiet place, read a book, swim, hike, jog, or whatever helps you to clear your mind, body, and soul. Soon there will be so much going through your head and so many important decisions to be made, you'll need to keep as many distractions at bay as you can.

There are also some administrative issues you need to tend to—most notably, setting up your business. This isn't hard. In most cases, it involves spending just a short time at the Secretary of State's office and a visit to your federal office building. When you arrive, you'll fill out a form with ownership and contact information along with the structure you've chosen for your business—LLC, a sole proprietorship, corporation, etc. For something as simple as foodservice, an LLC is common. Research your options and discuss them with your accountant. You'll pay a filing fee, submit the application, and wait for approval. Later, you may need to return, as you'll also need a retail merchant certificate, federal and state tax IDs, and maybe other miscellaneous documents for your state. But for the most part, that's it. Just remember: The people who work in the offices of the Secretary of State, *et al*, are paid to answer your questions and instruct you on the process. It's their job. Make sure you're clear on everything you need to do from an administrative standpoint to get your business up and running. Ask as many questions as you want and make the most of your visit(s).

> **TIP**
> Unless you're dealing with some intricate ownership structures and operating agreements, you don't need an attorney to incorporate your business, so save the cash.

This is also the time to pinpoint a location and secure financing. (For more information, refer to Chapter 5, "Getting Your Finances in Order," and Chapter 6, "Location, Location, Location.")

12–6 Months to Opening Day

By the time you're a year to six months out from opening, you should have found an operating space in the right part of town and be in the process of either negotiating your lease (with the help of your broker) or purchasing the property. After that, there will be a flurry of meetings with vendors. You'll also settle on a bank and choose a credit card–processing company.

> **TIP**
> Don't wait until the last minute to shop for food suppliers, professional services, point-of-sale systems, banks, and so forth. Give yourself plenty of time to shop and compare to get the best possible deals.

Choosing Your Food Vendors

Perhaps your most important task during this period is to meet with various food distributors (also called *broadline suppliers*, meaning they can provide just about everything for your operation)—folks like Sysco, U.S. Foods, Gordon Food Service, along with any regional or local players. These people will be falling all over themselves bringing you food for you to sample, rebate deals, and other incentives in the hopes you'll make them your "preferred" vendor.

Don't just meet with one vendor. Contact at least two and maybe three of the major players and discuss your concept and menu with them. At this point, focus on your order guide (your grocery list) and have them price it out. While you're waiting on that, take a trip to your local warehouse clubs and restaurant food suppliers—Sam's Club, Costco, BJ's, Restaurant Depot, or whatever is similar in your area. That way, you'll be armed with enough information to get the best pricing you can from everyone.

> **TIP**
> Now's not a bad time to decide whether you want to be a Coke or a Pepsi establishment. These companies may offer you a financial incentive to contract your business, so meet with the reps and see what's on the table.

As you meet from the reps from these various companies, keep these points in mind:

- These companies want your business...so make them work for it! It's not unheard of for food service companies to offer access to menu consultants and kitchen and dining room designers. You may be able to get them to pay for professionally printed menus, dishwasher, signage, or a host of other goodies. Just remember: In exchange, you'll have to agree to give them a large percentage of your business. Nobody's so altruistic they'll give you something for nothing!
- Find out if there are any food shows coming up. These wonderful events—conventions, really—showcase hundreds of vendors. These vendors represent every food and beverage category you can think of, complete with

Chapter 7: A Sample Timeline to Opening Day

on-site cooking and all the samples you can taste. There are also paper product, packaging, and even some equipment dealers at these shows. Your food rep will be in attendance, meeting and greeting his or her accounts and happily filling orders. In addition, breakout sessions held by industry personnel cover best practices, highlight industry trends, and demonstrate the latest cooking techniques for hot new items. Even if you're still months away from opening, it can't hurt to attend a few of these. You'll see what's happening and meet the brokers who work for the manufacturers in conjunction with the suppliers.

- Unless you're getting cash up front, avoid contracts longer than one year. Coke and Pepsi will likely ask for multi-year deals, as will your broadline suppliers and credit card–processing company. Instead, insist on a year-to-year arrangement. This allows you freedom of movement and the ability to negotiate smaller fees as your business grows over time.
- If your broadline supplier tries to pull you into a discussion about chemicals, cleaning products, kitchen equipment, or furniture, don't bite. For now, keep the discussions strictly about food. At this stage of the game, you'll want to buy food from the food people and equipment from the equipment people. The supplier's markup on these items can be astronomical and you may save a lot of money buying elsewhere.

> **TIP**
>
> While you're costing out your order guide, price fresh produce. Pre-sliced tomatoes, onions, and so forth are available from suppliers but cost a lot more. Plan on buying a tomato and onion slicer and slice your own. It'll be better and cheaper to present them in all their imperfect—yet fresh—glory. That being said, there are some items you may opt to buy frozen. French fries and onion rings come to mind. If you can't pull off a decent house-made version of these staples, there's no shame in using a top-shelf frozen product.

Ideally, for ease of ordering and streamlining of paperwork, it'd be great if a single vendor could handle everything—in other words, if you could have an exclusive relationship with one vendor. (And the rep, of course, will tell you this makes sense because it means more commission dollars for them.) In the nearly 20 years we've been operating, however, we've had an exclusive contract only one time, and that was for just one year. Unfortunately, at some time or another, we've had service, quality, or price issues with every supplier we've used. We've found being able to ditch one in favor of another if need be ensures the best competitive edge. Indeed, switching vendors for certain items may immediately save hundreds of dollars a week. These days, we buy a little bit from two or three different vendors and watch their pricing to keep everyone on their toes. We also buy our own produce directly from a wholesaler rather than a supplier. This saves between $500 and $700 per month and gives us the added benefit of being able to look over everything and select our own before we buy it. The downside is it's on our own time. Driving, loading, delivering, and unloading presents a cost factor, but it's more than made up with the savings. Now this is what works for us as a *single unit* operation. As you scale or franchise, it's probably better to have a primary vendor, but there should be a corresponding savings based on your larger purchasing volume.

> **TIP**
>
> Construct your final menu so you can purchase your products from virtually any vendor, including the wholesale clubs. If the butter, flour, oil, ketchup, or whatever is cheaper somewhere else, why pay more?

Buying Local

If you can buy everything local and market yourself as such, and you feel doing so helps your business, by all means do it! Nothing beats the satisfaction of supporting your local economy with traceable, accountable products and building relationships with fellow local businesspeople. You will have particularly good luck with local butchers, bread makers, craft brewers, and farmers. (If you live in a cold climate, produce purchases will understandably be a seasonal affair.) Cost everything out. If the price of meat you buy locally comes in the same, less, or even a little more than a broadline supplier, then go for it. If the math doesn't work for you, then don't.

Like anything else, this works only if your local providers offer good service and consistency. For a time, we bought tomatoes from a local farmer. In the beginning, the quality and prices were great. But after a while, the quality fell off, and we couldn't get proper quantities. Plus, they started showing up late for deliveries—and twice were a no-call, no-show. Sure, it felt good buying tomatoes straight from the farm, but obviously for business reasons we had to part ways.

Chapter 7: A Sample Timeline to Opening Day

Another time, the "local" owner of a chain bakery approached me about buying buns from him. He assured me we wouldn't get bread any fresher unless we made our own. Agreeing, I told him if he could guarantee me between 1,500 and 2,000 buns a week and the price worked, we might have a deal. His eyes lit up. He told me to come to his store the next day to check out his operation and that he'd have some fresh samples to try. When I arrived for the samples, he explained that my batch had mistakenly been overcooked and asked if we could reschedule. "Sure," I said. "No problem." Then, as we made small talk, he mentioned that if we partnered, he'd need to invest in an extra bread slicer—unless I didn't mind slicing my own buns. I thought, "Why the fuck would I want to slice 2,000 buns a week?" Why that was brought up, I don't know. Equipment was his issue, not ours. Next, we got to the topic of price. I was a little disappointed to find out I wouldn't be saving much, but I figured, hey, the guy's around the corner and the bread would damn near still be warm when it arrived. He apologized for the SNAFU and offered to bring a batch over to our store the next day.

Well, he did come the next day, but didn't have any bread with him. He said there had been some confusion on the part of the baker, and our samples hadn't gotten made. He was terribly sorry, and would bring some by the following day. "No thanks," I said. As nice as it sounded to have fresh-baked buns made just for us right down the street, working with this guy posed a clear risk. His crew couldn't follow directions, he needed another slicer he didn't sound too keen on investing in, and his price wasn't any better than what we were currently paying. What if they messed up our order or failed to deliver it on a Friday? I could hardly run a burger business without any damn *buns*. It wasn't worth it to leave the current supplier, with whom I had a great relationship and who offered a consistent product and no-headache delivery. I wound up sticking with "Big Bread," and sadly but unsurprisingly the local guy wound up closing his store about a year later.

What constitutes "local"? The bakery I mentioned was part of a chain owned by a local. So was it "local"? If an out of state chain opens in your city, but it buys everything from surrounding farms, can it claim to be "local"? The answer is yes and yes. In my opinion, you're local if you pay local taxes, hire local people, and live locally.

Somewhere in all that commerce is room for everyone I'm sure. The real winner anyway is your local department of revenue.

Mapping Out Your Kitchen

If you've secured your space and have your floor plan in hand, you'll want to get an idea of your kitchen layout and the equipment you'll need. This is an important step. Map things out carefully, as you'll only get one shot to get it right! You can always get professional help with design if you feel it's necessary. Some sources include your broadline supplier, equipment dealer, and private consultants.

> **NOTE**
> Your space may not be perfect—none of ours have ever been ideal—but you and your crew will eventually develop a rhythm and be able to work with what you have.

Signing Up with a Bank and a Merchant Services Company

It's also time to sign up with a bank and a merchant services company to process credit cards. Your bank can be local or national—whatever your preference. With your bank, take into account proximity, fees, ATMs, etc. It's not a bad idea to stick with one bank for all your needs and start developing that personal relationship that may make a difference down the road.

With regard to merchant services, there are many companies that do this, including your bank. It's worth shopping around to compare fees. (Yes, you pay fees for the convenience of being able to accept credit cards!) The process for setting this up is the same regardless of what type of business you're in—a restaurant, a landscaping company, or what have you—and it's fairly easy to do. Avoid entering into a long contract if you can. You'll come across better pricing as your business grows.

> **NOTE**
> I recommend you accept cards. Cash only is great too, but you exclude a few customers who enjoy the convenience or have perks attached to their bank cards. Then again, by accepting only cash, you can save thousands of dollars on fees. If you go the cash-only route, investigate putting an ATM in your space—problem solved.

Chapter 7: A Sample Timeline to Opening Day

6–3 Months to Opening Day

By the time you're six months out or less, you should have a lease agreement in place and at *least* three months of rent concession to cover your buildout time, permit issues, delays, slowdowns, and any other bullshit that can go down. (Ideally you want to open during this grace period with no rent payment if possible.) You should also have secured contractors for your buildout and have a solid plan. Next, you're ready to narrow down your equipment list. Finally, it'll be time to settle on a logo and to shop for signage.

Building Out Your Space

When it comes to your buildout, there are restaurant specialists you can use. Alternatively, you can be your own general contractor and hire the carpenters, plumbers, and electricians yourself. Your peers may have recommendations; if so, pay attention. They'll be brutally honest about who's good and who to avoid. Get estimates, shop, and compare. Once that's done, you'll be ready to start your buildout.

If you're building out a vanilla box, (not advised for first-timers), your construction could take any number of turns. It could take half a year or more, which is why you should find a closed restaurant instead! If you have landed in a former restaurant, depending on the condition, you may not have much to do buildout-wise. Your exhaust hood and fire-suppression system should already be in place. All you'll need to do is have it cleaned and inspected. Plumbing and electrical should already be to code, but may need tweaking or updating depending on your needs. You may even have some equipment and furniture left behind by the former tenant, which you can use as you see fit. If you're lucky, it may be that the dining room and bathrooms only need a fresh coat of paint. If you find there's more to it, then you and your contractor will want to get moving as soon as you've signed the lease and have the keys.

Regardless of whether your buildout is simple or complicated, you'll want to keep these points in mind:

- The health department will want your floor plan and will contact you with any concerns about the layout. Wait for final approval of your plan before you start anything! If you're unsure of any ADA requirements, what can and can't be "grandfathered," or any new codes, now is the time to get that ironed out.
- Work top-down to make sure your roof and any HVAC equipment is safe and sound and in working order.

- Address any repairs that are the landlord's responsibility—such as parking lot resurfacing, roof repairs, etc.—right away. That way, they won't cause interruptions after you open.
- Set up your audio and security systems while the ceiling is open and the electrician is doing his or her thing. We made the mistake of waiting too long to make final decisions about cameras and music. As a result, the alarm company and audio installers removed big sections of freshly painted ceiling tiles to run their wires *after* the lights and fans had been installed. The result was a ceiling full of dusty handprints—which yours truly had to clean up.

> **TIP**
>
> Install a working alarm system with a panic button. Security cameras are also a must. We use a local alarm company. They answer their own phones here in town, not in another state. And the installation and service is top-notch.

- If you're in a free-standing building, assess the condition of the exterior lighting and parking lot (if you have one). Freshen up any paint or landscaping. The neighborhood and passers-by will love to see your progress, and will be excited to see what's coming next.

Narrowing Down Your Equipment List

Now's the time to narrow down your equipment list. It will likely include the following, depending on your concept:

- Ovens
- Fryers
- Grills
- Coolers
- Pots and pans
- Utensils
- Work tables

You may also need a proper exhaust hood, fan, and return air system. Be warned: This can be very expensive. Around here, it's estimated at roughly $1,000 to $1,500 per foot of hood length.

Chapter 7: A Sample Timeline to Opening Day

Creating Your Logo

Every business needs a logo. What your business *doesn't* need, however, is a logo designed by your brother-in-law using clip art he found on the Internet.

You absolutely should hire a professional graphic designer to create a logo for your business. You'll be competing with well-established local and national brands, so you'll want to meet them evenly here. A well-thought-out, professionally designed logo will help you do just that. If professional and polished is what you're going for—and it should be—then hiring a designer is money well spent.

As you're working with the designer, have that person meet you in your space. Let him or her soak in the vibe and feel of your place. This will help you convey your brand's personality, whether it's fun, gourmet, casual, family-oriented, sports-themed, rustic, etc. Then turn the designer loose. Odds are he or she will return with several awesome ideas. From there, you can select and fine-tune the final look.

As you develop your logo, keep these points in mind:

- Create a logo that's easy to read and easy to pronounce. Generally, it's best if it contains no more than two words.
- So-called "food colors," like red, yellow, black, and white, are tried and true.
- Don't get overly fancy or abstract. You're not opening a clothing store or nightclub.

Shopping for Signage

Your sign is key. A reputable sign company will take your newly designed logo and create any kind of sign to fit your needs. Be sure to obtain quotes from several companies before you pull the trigger.

How big should it be? As big as possible, in my opinion. Signage that's too small is one of my pet peeves. Nothing's more annoying than having to squint at a little bitty sign with some weird-assed font. The proprietor is making me work too hard figuring out where I am!

Depending on the covenants set forth by your landlord and/or your city, you may have to work within certain parameters. I get that. But if you have a bit of leeway, get the biggest sign you can. If you're in an auto-centric city, like I am, people driving by your restaurant should be able to easily read your sign, whether it's on a pole in the parking lot, on the building itself, or on an awning.

A small sign isn't just hard to read. It also conveys timidity. Unless you're a super high-end exclusive operation or in a dense, urban environment, that 12×12–inch brass plate won't fly. You want to boldly announce yourself to the public. A big sign shouts confidence. It says, "Hello! Come in!"

3 Months to Opening Day

With three months to go, your space should be coming together. Soon, it'll be time to obtain and install your equipment. This is one thing I always enjoy, the toys!

Equipment

When the time comes to obtain your equipment, you'll have three choices:

- You can lease new equipment.
- You can buy new equipment.
- You can buy used equipment from a dealer or at an auction.

Our first equipment-buying experience was with the catering business. When visiting showrooms of local dealers, I experienced sticker shock over what amounted to an oversized refrigerator costing almost $2,000! Looking at the ovens, prep tables, and everything else on my list, it took us mere minutes to realize that buying new would easily set us back $10,000. Leasing was an option, but who wanted another bill every month? Instead, I decided I'd be "smart" and buy everything used. What difference did pre-owned equipment make as long as it worked? I found a used-equipment dealer and got coolers, shelving, a small freezer, and several other items to get going. I was proud of all the money I saved, and everything worked just fine.

After six months or so, I needed another reach-in cooler. This time around, I got wind of an on-site restaurant auction at a local steakhouse, seemingly the victim of a neighborhood losing population to the nearby developing suburbs. Everything was for sale, from the bar fixtures and lighting to the kitchen and office equipment. There were huge walk-in coolers and freezers, a dishwasher, exhaust hoods, and "smalls"—stuff like utensils, bowls, pans, and so on. We set our sights on the cooler we needed and a manual meat slicer.

The auction began and they eventually got around to the cooler and slicer we wanted. After bidding with a few others, we won both items. The cooler—in far better shape than the one we had bought from the used-equipment dealer for $800 just a few months earlier (and which we had thought was a bargain, considering it would have been $1,500

Chapter 7: A Sample Timeline to Opening Day

new)—was $300. And the meat slicer, which would have been about $700 new, was $90. "Damn!" I thought. "Why didn't we do this earlier?"

A few months later, while at another auction, I ran into the owner of the used-equipment store. Kelly was an older gentleman—in his 70s, at least—and the nicest guy you could meet. He was there along with half a dozen other dealers, private resellers, and new and veteran restaurant owners. We joked about how much money I'd be saving today driving past his store and buying at the auction. He didn't disagree. Kelly shared the key to his success. "Here's what nice about the equipment business," he began. "You gotta come see me when you open," he said, pointing to the ceiling. Then, pointing toward the floor, he continued, "and you gotta come see me when you close." It made perfect sense.

When a restaurant closes, the owner has only a few options with his furniture and equipment. One option is to sell everything privately and probably get the most money, but that means moving bulky, heavy appliances and storing them until they're sold. Another option is to sell everything to a dealer, who comes over, sizes it up, and makes a cash offer on the spot. This will yield the least amount of money (10 to 15 cents on the dollar), but they'll make a deal quickly and haul everything away. The third option is to consign with an auction company. If a restaurant is opening in a few weeks and absolutely needs a stove or griddle, doesn't want to spend on new, and there aren't any current auctions, the used-equipment dealer may be the only resource. The dealer, meanwhile, *always* buys at a discount. As long as he's cheaper than new, he can set his own prices. He does not lose.

So which should you do—lease, buy new, buy used from a dealer, or buy used from an auction? Obviously, I'd advise you to buy used from auction whenever you can. You'll find especially good deals on seating and tables for your dining room, certain office items, and various small wares. Hot-line equipment such as grills, stoves, fryers, broilers, are also good finds, as well as coolers and freezers, which are generally very durable.

> **TIP**
>
> Coolers and freezers at an auction should be running and have a thermometer inside to verify temperature. Look for a paper cup of water inside, which should be cold or frozen, depending on whether it's a cooler or freezer.

If the auction is for a restaurant that was part of a national chain, there's a good chance the operator bought brand-new equipment (often a requirement of the franchisor).

Those are where you'll find the best deals. One of our best scores was at an auction for a chili chain that closed after less than two years. We snagged a slide-top freezer and a nifty trash receptacle for our dining room, both nearly new, saving us at least $800. You may have similar luck if the restaurant being liquidated was one of those "cute" independent places. In that case, someone may have convinced the operator they needed a lot of top-of-the-line appliances.

There are obvious reasons to buy new equipment. If there are certain pieces of equipment crucial to your menu—for example, if you're opening a donut shop and you need a donut fryer—then it might make sense to buy new. You want to make sure you spend the money in the right places. As an added bonus, buying new means you get the peace of mind that comes with a warranty as well as help with delivery and setup. If you're catering or the public can't see your kitchen, your equipment can be as mismatched, dented, and ugly as you can stand, so feel free to buy used. As long as it can be cleaned up and does its job, save as much money up front as you can.

What about brands? Certain brands have a better reputation than others. But I've had problems with "good" (read: expensive) brands within a year, and no issues for almost 10 years with no-name brand equipment that came out of a garage and cost $100. Ask dealers as much as you can about the items and talk with other operators about what's worked for them. Often, it's trial and error.

> **TIP**
>
> Plan to buy the biggest grills and ovens you can fit in your kitchen. If you're betting on yourself to win, you need to be able to serve as many people as possible! If there's room for a 48-inch grill, why buy the 36-inch model? You'll wish you had the bigger one when the kitchen gets backed up with all those orders!

Putting Your Kitchen Together

As you're putting your kitchen together, make sure your measurements and floor plan are solidly in place. One thing to remember is that all your hot-line equipment has to fit under your hood. If you've assumed a former restaurant space and the hood isn't big enough, which has happened to us, you'll need to make adjustments. In some cases, you can add on to the existing hood with corresponding fire-suppression to code. In other cases, you may have to rethink your setup and be creative with your equipment.

Chapter 7: A Sample Timeline to Opening Day

When we were preparing to relocate the burger joint into a bigger location, we spent some time in the new kitchen before we moved one damn grill. We got a bunch of empty boxes and crates of varying sizes to simulate our equipment and moved them around into possible layouts and various heights to figure out how to best position our real equipment for maximum convenience and efficiency.

> **NOTE**
> Often, you'll only get one shot to set everything up. Think it through and look at all possibilities. Once it's in, unless you want to reroute gas and water lines you're stuck with it.

If you're opening a quick-serve restaurant, also put some thought into how you want to set up the counter area where your customers will place and/or pick up their orders. Just like your kitchen, set it up for maximum efficiency and flow for your front-of-house team, who'll be buzzing like bees filling orders while working the cash register.

1 Month to Opening Day

You've bought and installed your fixtures and equipment. You've finalized inventory. From a legal standpoint, you're ready to do business. Any issues with the Department of Revenue, Board of Health, or the Fire Marshal, as well as any county or city codes, should have been corrected, re-inspected, and approved. Your business and workman's comp insurance is also in place.

So what's next? Here are some of the things you should be focused on now:

- **Interviewing and hiring your staff:** For more on this, read Chapter 8, "Hiring and Firing."
- **Setting up your point-of-sale (POS) system:** If you have an electronic POS system, make sure it's online and linked to the proper bank accounts. Perform a test run.
- **Handling necessary maintenance work:** If your space was already a restaurant, clean grease the traps and snake all drains, toilets, and urinals.
- **Cleaning the exhaust hood and fire-suppression system:** If your space came with an exhaust hood and fire-suppression system, have it thoroughly cleaned. While you're at it, replace the belt in your exhaust fan. Otherwise, you'll find yourself in a predicament like the one I was in on the first day we opened. The exhaust fan stopped working, sending billows of thick, greasy smoke

throughout our tiny dining room. Thankfully, it was around 2 p.m., so lunch was over, and the place was basically empty. Still, I had no idea what had happened or what to do. I tracked down our handyman, who shimmied onto the roof and opened the fan, revealing the problem: a broken fan belt. He told me I could grab one at any auto-supply store and it wouldn't be a problem putting it back on. Fortunately, he was right. True, we hadn't missed too many sales, but it embarrassing and a real buzzkill.

- **Getting set up with an exterminator:** Call your local pest-control outfit and have the place treated. Then set a schedule for routine treatments.
- **Setting up an account with an oil-recovery business:** This company will provide and maintain your grease dumpster. They buy spent oil for recycling, so you should also receive a monthly check.
- **Getting set up for trash removal:** You will likely have several choices, and most will be pretty competitive. Once you choose your vendor, they'll help you decide what size dumpster to use and frequency of trash pickup. After you get going, you can always get a larger or smaller dumpster or change the frequency of pickups.

> **NOTE**
>
> Despite what you may have seen in the movies, it's unlikely you'll deal with organized crime with respect to your trash collection. However it's not unheard of. When I lived back east, there was an operator in the Tri-State area who opened in an unconventional neighborhood and was made to feel unwelcome. Allegedly, their trash company suddenly increased fees and added surcharges at which the owner balked. There were no broken thumbs or lead pipes to kneecaps when the restaurant refused the shakedown; the trash company simply stopped picking up the trash. Daily citations from the city piled up, as did the mounds of rotting garbage. A restaurant generates large amounts of trash, so what were they to do? There was no competitor to turn to and the municipality was no help. What finally became of that situation, I have no idea.

- **Generating buzz:** Send out announcements and press releases to your local media, including food and restaurant bloggers. Also get your social media posts rolling and distribute menus in office buildings, apartment buildings, and residences in a one- or two-mile radius around your new place. Note, however,

Chapter 7: A Sample Timeline to Opening Day

that you may not have to do much. It may well be that the local food scene already has you on their radar and are eagerly anticipating a new place to eat!

1 Week to Opening Day

One week to opening day! No doubt, the butterflies are kicking in. You're nervous, but the rush is like no other.

If all official agencies have given you the OK to operate, and you're absolutely, positively certain you're ready to do business, it's time to order your inventory. (Don't do this unless you're 100% sure. You don't want $5,000 worth of perishables on hand if it turns out there's an issue that will take weeks to remedy.)

Before opening, you'll want to have a dry run of sorts. Invite all your friends and family to a private opening (or two). Cook everything and give a narrow window for the gathering so as many people come in at once as possible (just like it will be in real life). Have everyone on your staff practice on the POS system to confirm they know what they're doing and the equipment works as it should—i.e., kitchen printers, Internet, etc.

It's easy in the scramble of pre-opening to forget things will break down. Nevertheless, they will, and it's best to be ready when it happens. To that end, put together a list of contractors and repair people so you won't have to track them down in the heat of the moment if something goes wrong. Ask your peers who they've used and who they trust. If you can, get two or three names for each discipline. Assemble their information on a single sheet of paper, laminate it, and post in a conspicuous area in the office or in the kitchen. That way, anyone can contact them if you or the manager aren't around. This list can include (but is not limited to) the following:

- Electrician
- Plumbing, sewer, and drain repair
- HVAC
- IT/POS support
- Equipment and exhaust hood repair people
- Locksmith

In addition, keep a toolbox on hand for routine maintenance. Leaky faucets and running toilets are annoying and ever-so-quietly steal from your bottom line, so fix them ASAP. Ditto any lightbulbs that need replacing and locks that need changing. Here's what I keep in my toolbox (along with a hand truck or dolly at the back door):

- A drill with various drivers and bits
- Screwdrivers
- Hammer
- Rubber mallet
- Assorted pliers
- Monkey wrenches (for gas and water lines)
- Teflon tape
- Electrical tape
- Duct tape (yes!)
- Allen keys
- Flashlights
- Wood shims
- Lock de-icer
- Graphite powder for lubing door locks
- WD40 or similar silicon-type spray
- Nails and screws
- Batteries

> **CAUTION**
>
> The more fixes you can do yourself, the better. Just don't overshoot your skill level. Otherwise, you'll pay. Oh, how you'll pay.

Opening Day

Congratulations! You've done it. This is the day you've been waiting for. All your hard work has turned your idea into reality, and you're ready to introduce it to the world.

When you open to the public, they will tolerate—even expect—a few hiccups, so relax and go with the flow. Your main goal is to get through this first day, open to close. You can laugh about all the first-day craziness later.

> **CAUTION**
>
> If you're a caterer, don't expect much in the way of fanfare on opening day. Instead, plan to hit the streets hard to let the world know you're ready to serve them. Sure, you can get pre-orders before you go live, but don't be surprised if your first few weeks are quiet.

Chapter 7: A Sample Timeline to Opening Day

What Day Should You Open?

We've always preferred to open on a Monday or a Tuesday. You're likely to draw a smaller crowd, which gives you a chance to ease into things and work out mistakes before the weekend onslaught.

Still, a few people prefer to open on a weekend, under the theory this will ensure plenty of buzz, a full parking lot, and a line out the door. If you go this route, God help you—especially if you are new to this business. I would attempt this only if I was working with the most seasoned of people, and even then I'd be leery. We know an operator who decided to open on a Saturday, in the spring, in a fantastic area. It was a highly anticipated addition to the neighborhood, so naturally, on that first day, they were packed beyond belief. But the strategy backfired. The wait times for a quick-service concept grew from minutes to hours, they ran out of inventory early in the day, and the whole thing was a mess. This wasn't the introduction they wanted and some held it against them for a long time.

> **NOTE**
> Some restaurants will have a *soft opening*, meaning they open for limited hours or days before having their grand opening. Essentially, it's a chance to get their shit together before the crowd comes—and it's not the worst idea ever!

Making Sure You're Fully Stocked

Obviously, on opening day, everything in the kitchen should be in working order. In addition, you should make sure you're fully stocked. As best you can, have everything on your menu available for guests to order. If you've haven't rushed to open, this shouldn't be an issue.

A restaurant opened in our area at a great location. It had a beautiful dining room, a solid menu, a great bar, and a family-friendly vibe. We stopped in a few weeks after opening and were warmly welcomed by the staff. We sat down and looked over the menu. Everything was deliciously described, and we were eager to try several dishes. The only problem was, half the menu was unavailable. In fact, the first thing our server mentioned was what *wasn't* available on the menu. I'm sure there was a defensible reason these items were MIA. Maybe certain recipes needed tweaking. Maybe the delivery driver was late that day and inventory just wasn't in. But this was almost a month into their opening!

> **TIP**
>
> If your menu isn't finalized but you need to open and get sales going, print temporary menus of what you *can* serve and present a finalized menu later. The public will never know what's missing because they never saw it in the first place. Plus, it's great marketing. Your servers can tout your awesome new menu items that are "coming next week!"

Making Sure You're Fully Staffed

To some extent, you can control your inventory issues ahead of time. What you *can't* control—whether it's the first day or your fifth anniversary—is the flakiness of your staff.

Opening day for the burger joint was set for a Monday at 11 a.m. I was slated to work with the two cooks we hired. Two hours before we were scheduled to open, I got a call from one of the cooks, informing me he wasn't coming in and was no longer interested in the job. There we were, down to one cook and me—10 hours a day, seven days a week. In a few weeks, we found additional cooks, but not until the two of us nearly dropped dead from exhaustion. Here's hoping this doesn't happen to you!

Taking Stock

On opening day, you might serve a dozen people and wind up with a grand total of $100. Alternatively, you might see a non-stop run for five hours straight. However it goes, get through the day as best you can. Keep these points in mind:

- Welcome your guests, introduce yourself as the owner, and thank them for coming in.
- Note patterns, mistakes, and possible improvements to service and delivery, including phone orders for carry-out if applicable.
- Pay attention to how things flow in the kitchen with your menu.
- Note how the dining-room arrangement is working.
- Determine whether you have too many people on the clock (or not enough).

Remember: You've made it to the point most people only dream about. You may be broke, you may have maxed out all your credit, and you may owe people a bunch of money. But you're here! You're just getting started. And *getting* open is infinitely easier than *staying* open. For more on that, read on…

Chapter 7: A Sample Timeline to Opening Day

> **TIP**
>
> As the owner, it's critical you be present on opening day—and on most days after that, especially early on. No one is going to be able to run your place like you. Only by being around will you be able to pick up on the little things, like whether you're going through too much soap, ketchup, napkins, towels, etc. (the stuff you pay for but that doesn't make money). Likewise, you can only determine whether the kitchen is weighing out portions, controlling waste, and so on if you're on site. The more you're around in the beginning, the better things will run!

Chapter 8

Hiring and Firing

When you're an owner-operator in the food service business, by default you will earn a *de-facto* degree in sociology. Among your employees, you will observe human behaviors and habits you may not have noticed when you were an employee or even supervisor in another work environment. Your new status as a business owner will test your patience, temper, and leadership abilities. You'll often be irritated, but things will never be dull, and you will never be bored. With your newly developed superhero-level mental powers, you'll quickly sniff out closely held frailties and flaws in your fellow citizens' character and work ethic.

You'll notice these things with a new, laser-like acuity for one reason and one reason only: These people are being paid on *your* dime. In fact, labor will be your second-biggest expense after food. When the money comes from your own dwindling checking account, you tend to pay a little more attention when they're 10 minutes late, on the phone, or take too many breaks. After all, you're the one who cashed out your savings, accepted a $25,000 loan from your in-laws, took out a second mortgage on your home, and maxed out your credit cards to start your business.

The first person I officially hired was also the first person I had to fire—although in this case, it wasn't her fault. It was a friend of ours who'd left another job to give me a hand with the catering business. Our agreement had been I'd pay her a weekly salary (which, it turned out, was way too high). In exchange, she would handle paperwork, answer the phones, and help me in the kitchen.

When we outgrew our original location and bought the building, I was out of cash. I couldn't afford her anymore. The best I could offer was a part-time hourly position, paying her every two weeks. It was either that or nothing. Needless to say, she wasn't thrilled with the news and financially couldn't accept the part-time offer. But after an honest discussion, she understood my position. I felt I'd let her down, but in the end, the business was experiencing growing pains, and I had to do what I had to do. Fortunately, she landed on her feet a short time later.

Since then I've hired and laid off or fired scores—and I mean *scores*—of people. I've discovered hiring people is easy, and if deserved, firing them is even easier. I've fired people first thing in the morning, in the middle of a shift, over the phone, and even in their own front yard. I am completely at ease with firing people. If anything, I'm usually upset I didn't do it sooner. As you embark on your restaurant business, you'll need to be equally at ease both hiring and firing your staff.

> **NOTE**
>
> A startup is filled with casualties, and the owner is often the last one standing. If you have to let people go and work it damn near by yourself for a time, so be it.

Filling the Ranks

So what positions do you need to fill? At a minimum, the following:

- Cooks
- Servers (or cashiers, if you're running a quick-service operation)

In addition to these, you may also need a host or hostess as well as bussers, dishwashers, and bartenders if you're running a full-service restaurant.

Your cooks are the backbone of your business, and are generally the most stable of the group. You'll want to pay them competitively—and for the good ones who stick around, you'll want to pay them even better. Your front-of-house staff may be more volatile. It could consist of a mix of part-timers, students, and people brand new to the workforce.

> **NOTE**
>
> During an interview, people will tell you want you want to hear. When you ask them how many times they were late at their current job, or what would they do if they saw someone stealing, or how they resolved an issue with a very difficult customer, they will say all the right things. Some will be telling the truth, others will be lying. You won't know which is which until they start.

Chapter 8: Hiring and Firing

> **CAUTION**
> Never hire anyone without calling their previous employers. And call *all* of them. Ask, "Would you hire this person again? How was their job performance and what are they like to work with?" Listen carefully to their responses and let them talk as long as necessary. This is about the extent of due diligence possible with something as straightforward as foodservice. It isn't high security government work. Cross your fingers and hope for the best. If the applicant is currently employed at another restaurant, be wary when a manager offers *too much* praise. They could be looking to unload a headache, and your place is as good as any.

Do You Need a Manager?

In the beginning, you may not need a manager—mainly because you need to figure out how your business works yourself before you can show anyone else how run it for you. Eventually, however—after you've learned the ins and outs, you know what the numbers look like, and you're sure you can afford it—hiring a manager will likely be the right thing to do. This person is second in command, and will represent the business to patrons and to the community. He or she is integral to keeping things humming. There are dozens of books with advice for hiring good people, but in your gut, you know you're looking for honesty, integrity and a strong work ethic. (That goes for all your employees, not just the manager.)

Even if you land the best manager on Earth, remember: That person is no substitute for you. Don't make the mistake of handing over the keys and checking out. The fact is, it's your business, and you need to be there to run it. If it closes, the manager won't be out anything; he or she can just find another job. For you, it will be another story altogether. It's your money on the craps table, not theirs!

Growing Your Staff

At first, you may not need a large staff—and you might not be able to afford one anyway. Then you might find yourself in an in-between phase, where you're busy enough to keep the place open and pay bills, but not busy enough to hire extra help. This is a frustrating period, because often, it means you're stuck putting in 12-, 16-, and 18-hour days. At the same time, you're working with a crew so thin that if somebody gets sick or suddenly quits, you're SOL and have to work even more. Some owners don't escape this netherworld of back-breaking work for months or even years.

> **TIP**
> Be prepared to work the line or the cash register—or maybe both—yourself. Depending on how much cash you have left after you open, you may be the only employee you can afford!

The solution, of course, is more revenue—more people coming through the door. The good news is, when you're finally busy enough and can hire those extra people, you'll have put in enough hours to know every ebb and flow of your operation. The bad news is, if you never get that "pop," you'll be held hostage in your own store, toiling away until your tipping point.

> **TIP**
> If you can afford it, staff a little more than you think you'll need after you open. Then pull back after you get into your routine and assess how many (or how few) people are actually required to make everything work. It's natural to want a cushion around you in the beginning, but after a while, you'll enjoy having as few people around as possible.

Your Labor Pool

There are generally two types of foodservice workers: those who have a choice in the matter and those who don't. If you can, opt for the former.

The best employees are those who enjoy providing good service. They take a genuine interest in the person in front of them. Moreover, they like working in the foodservice world. It's where they want to be. They thrive in the atmosphere and enjoy the pace of the restaurant industry. Whether they're lifers or just passing through, these are the individuals you want on your team. Cherish the good ones and treat them right.

> **NOTE**
> Good people want to work at a winning operation, but to have a winning operation, you need good people. It's a bit of a chicken-or-egg scenario, I know, but it's true.

Chapter 8: Hiring and Firing

What about those who *don't* have a choice in the matter? There's always a set of people in this industry who are on their second or third chances and frankly have nowhere else to go. Foodservice still embraces these people because there will *always* be work in the kitchen. We try to give everyone a shot, and yes, we have been burned. But we've been equally burned by people who supposedly "had it all together."

> **NOTE**
>
> There's no drug testing for the most part in the foodservice industry. If there were, there would be no foodservice industry. It moves too fast and it turns over too much. We draw the line on hiring certain felony offenders. At the same time, if we tossed out every application listing a DUI or public intoxication charge, we wouldn't last two minutes in the business. After we make the decision to hire someone, we warn them against coming to work drunk, high, or stupid. That's about all we can do.

When you are small, new, and unknown, you may not attract top-shelf front- and back-of-house staff. More than likely, you'll be dealing with younger people, part-time students, or folks with two and three jobs. Many of these people live paycheck to paycheck. Some may have issues with reliable transportation or suspended driver's licenses.

We've had more than our fair share of shenanigans, up to and including mutiny. But the longer we stayed in business, the easier it became to hire great people—some of who are still with us years later. As we began to show signs of permanence, our turnover decreased, and we saw an increase in the quality of applicants. That enabled us to be a little choosier when it came to who we brought on board.

> **NOTE**
>
> Especially when you are first starting out, you'll often come across people who act as if they're doing you a favor by working for you. I usually find this attitude among big-chain and franchise rejects. They couldn't work in a structured environment, so they attempt to loaf on the local, independent operator's dollar, assuming you'll put up with their shit and life will be a little easier. Fire these people the fastest.

Ignoring Stereotypes

We hire the people of the world because we serve the people of the world. Over the years, we've employed as broad a spectrum as you can get: Black, White, Latino, Asian, young, old, gay, straight, and ex-cons, both male and female. We've had great working relationships with them all and we've seen them all act a fucking fool. Every. Single. One.

Don't fall prey to stereotypes. What matters in this game is integrity and work ethic—things a person either has or doesn't. We look for friendly people who can use their brain, and we don't care what package they come in. We've been lucky over the years to work with some great people, even if only for a short time. And we've learned something from everybody.

Some of Our Brand Ambassadors

Of course, we haven't always been lucky with the people we hire and we've had our fair share of horror stories and bullshit. We had a cook who, after working for with us for nearly five years, suddenly suffer a meltdown one busy Saturday afternoon. For whatever reason, he began glaring out into the dining room from our open kitchen, singling out patrons in line or sitting down, and flipping them the bird. No instigation or rationale…just giving the finger to anyone who was unfortunate enough to be in his line of sight. Needless to say, no one found this amusing. Guests waiting on orders began cancelling them and asking for refunds. Others left while they were still in line. The cashiers pleaded with him to stop his crazy shit, but to no avail.

Finally, one of my employees called me at home to tell me what was going on. I peeled out of my driveway and rushed to the restaurant. By the time I arrived, he had calmed down. He was at work in the kitchen, mumbling under his breath. I pulled him off the line and we talked in the parking lot. He didn't have a coherent explanation for his behavior and we both knew I had no choice but to fire him on the spot. I asked for his key and told him I'd mail him his final check. No need to come back to the restaurant. I got the locks changed just in case he was a complete wacko and came back to start some shit. I hated to lose him—he was one of our best cooks—but did we have a choice in the matter?

Then there was the young man who, after attempting to vault over the swinging half-door attached to the front counter, fell flat on his face out into the dining room. A few people laughed, some even stood and clapped at his idiotic stunt. Embarrassed, he

Chapter 8: Hiring and Firing

made the executive decision to close the restaurant a half hour early. He refused service to everybody standing in line and wouldn't refill anyone's drinks. Basically, he kicked everybody out of the place. It was so bad that for most of the next morning, we got phone calls and e-mails, not to mention social media posts, about what happened. Erin and I played back the video from the night before and watched in horror.

> **NOTE**
>
> If you've spent enough time in your place, your regular guests will get to know you and what you stand for—and the fact you don't condone any craziness that goes down when you're absent. Hopefully, those people who are friends to your business will contact you when something's not right. That's one of the great things about being a local independent operator.

He was off that morning, so I went to his house. I needed to retrieve some T-shirts we were planning to sell in the restaurant, which he and his girlfriend were supposed to tie-dye. When I got there, I asked for the shirts. Then I brought up his performance from the previous evening and let him know he was fired. All I wanted to know was, why? Like the other guy, he had no logical answer.

We lost a lot of goodwill from this. There were some out-of-town guests, a travelling baseball team if I remember, in the restaurant that evening, and that was their introduction to our business. Unfortunately, other than offering an apology to callers and to anyone who read our social media, there wasn't much I could do. The damage was done. Still, I could only blame myself. We were only a month in our new location. He was fairly new and I shouldn't have left him to work a busy Saturday night without us until I had gotten to know him better. I let the fact he was a little older and had industry experience cloud my common sense.

Sometimes, you don't have a choice. You simply have to fire someone. When this happens, do it quickly and move on. Your crew will see you are serious and understand your place operates with rules. When you terminate people, don't feel too badly about it. No doubt, that person will move on to another job within days. Besides, they obviously didn't feel too badly about doing whatever it was they did to get fired. One more thing: If it turns out one of your employees has lied to or stolen from you, don't take it personally. Even if it's someone you liked and trusted, it's not personal. People are who they are, and they're going to do what they're going to do. They'll do the same if they work for you or Red Lobster. Don't let it get you down. Just move on.

> **NOTE**
>
> As the owner of a restaurant, be ready to encounter anything you can imagine. Expect to be interrupted during dinner at home, to have to suddenly get up from your table at a restaurant, to leave your kid's soccer or baseball game, or to get out of bed and drag yourself into work because of a no show or other problem. You can't control how the people who work for you are going to act, even if you've vetted them as thoroughly as possible or they've worked for you for a significant length of time. And you can't shuffle them off to HR because HR is you. *You* are the person who will deal with no-shows and requests for days off and pay raises.

General Tips

Here are some general tips for hiring and firing:

- Always accept employment applications, even if you aren't hiring. It's best to have a list of people to call if you need them as soon as possible. We've called people months after they filled out an application and had it work out beautifully.
- Don't overlook older or retired workers. Many can keep up with the younger crowd, and their dependability is often worth their weight in gold.
- Don't pay people on Friday. If you'll do, you'll find that your employees are often late on Saturday or disappear until Monday. Instead, pay people on Tuesday or Wednesday.
- It may be awhile before you assemble a decent team that's willing to stick around. Don't let that alarm you. Just stay patient, organized, and in charge. Eventually, you'll be blessed with a good crew that can run things to your standards.
- Take care of your good people as best you can. They're hard to find!
- Your leadership will set the tone for the whole establishment. If you are a tense hothead who doesn't trust anybody, that will be reflected in your staff. On the other hand, if you are too easygoing, let things slide, and operate with vague rules or procedures, then the people working for you will be the same way. Find some middle ground here.

Chapter 9

Marketing

mar·ket·ing

The action or business of promoting and selling products or services, including market research and advertising.

You may have the coolest spot, an awesome menu, and an A-1 staff. But if no one knows about it, well, you'll speak about those wonderful things in the past tense sooner than later. Like it or not, in addition to being a restaurateur, you must be a salesperson.

> **TIP**
> If you're not used to speaking with different types of people, it may feel overwhelming asking total strangers to spend money on your food and drinks, but there is no room for shyness in this business. People expect to be sold to, so sell to them. There's no better way to start than by being inside your restaurant as much as possible to personally greet your guests and talk about your menu.

Marketing Channels

There are all kinds of ways to market your business. These include the following old-school methods:

- **Radio:** Especially in the beginning, radio advertising is an affordable option.
- **TV:** TV commercials can still get you great bang for your buck. Advertising on TV has a far greater reach than what people assume, even in the social media age. This is a medium we are definitely planning to explore in the future.
- **Print:** Certain print media can be effective, but be prepared to spend. To get a worthwhile return on investment, you'll need multiple ads over a period of time—and that adds up.

> **NOTE**
>
> We ran print ads in a local newsweekly after opening the burger joint, with some success. But what our account executive told us was true: Your print ads need to be seen at least six times by regular readers to get the most impact. For what it's worth, in our case, there did appear to be an uptick between weeks four and six of a campaign.

In addition, you have the Internet. These days, you'll find that for better or for worse, the World Wide Web—specifically, social media—will do most of your marketing for you. And the best part is, social media is *free*.

> **TIP**
>
> Of course, it should go without saying you should have a website with the requisite accoutrements. Get professional help here if it's in the budget.

Social Media

Back when we were catering, Yellow Pages ads were still popular—often a necessity. They were also expensive. We had a tiny 2×2–inch one-color ad that ran somewhere in the neighborhood of $200 per month. That was a tough check to write, but it counted right up there with the electricity and mortgage. (Besides, you didn't have much choice because it was tied to your phone bill. Obviously, a disconnected phone meant a worthless Yellow Pages ad.) Today, it's all about the Internet and social media. With social media, your brand lives and breathes in writing and pictures, accessible to millions of people in multiple formats, 24 hours a day!

You're certainly not obligated to use social media—plenty of restaurants don't. But it does offer an excellent way to market your business and engage with your customers. And again, it's free—assuming, of course, you handle it yourself rather than hire someone else to do it. At the very least, you should have a presence on Facebook, Twitter, and/or Instagram. These platforms really are the new phone books, print ads, flyers, and commercials. How active you choose to be and how you craft your online brand persona is up to you.

Just remember: Social media's great, but it should be the cherry on top of a satisfying guest experience. People will either come in—or come back—or they won't. What happens between the time they enter and the time they leave is the only thing that *really* matters. No computer application will ever replace a person-to-person connection in real life. That being said, if you operate a food truck or similar mobile cuisine, then you do need to be on social media, no matter what.

Choosing Your Platform

The social media landscape is ever-changing, and nobody knows what's next. At the moment, the big three seem to be Facebook, Twitter, and Instagram. It's not a bad idea to be on all three, but you might decide to focus on just one.

We have Twitter, Instagram, and an unofficial Facebook account, but when the time came to decide on our social media strategy, we decided to pick one platform. I personally can dedicate only so much time and energy to social media, so for now, one is enough for us. Twitter won for its brevity and ease of use, but it could just as easily have been Facebook. These days, there's software that enables you to quickly post across multiple platforms so your reach can be even broader.

Who Should Handle Your Social Media?

So who should handle your social media? You have a few options:

- **You:** You know your business and its inner workings better than anyone, so who better to shout to the world about it than you? There's no reason you can't be the person who handles this task—assuming you have the time. You can send out a post while you're cooking live in the restaurant itself or schedule a series of posts for the week while you're sitting on the toilet in Turks and Caicos.
- **A marketing company:** There are all sorts of marketing firms out there offering social media and other services custom-tailored to fit your business. If you go this route, expect to pay for it. Before you do, be sure you get a handle on what they're selling is worth what they're asking for it. (More about this later in this chapter.)
- **An employee:** A third option is to have a trusted employee or manager handle your social media accounts. This will definitely be cheaper than a marketing company, but still may have a cost attached.

For the mom-and-pop single or even multi-unit operator, I recommend handling your own social media. It's easy, it's free, it's fun, and you're in total control. You can post as little or as often as you like. In the end, whether you handle social media yourself or let someone else do it will come down to what your time is worth.

> **CAUTION**
>
> As an owner, I'd turn everything over to a professional with no ties to the business before I'd let an employee speak for my brand. This person is one controversial or misunderstood post away from creating a big-ass mess. Do you want that kind of publicity?

What Should You Share on Social Media?

I do the tweeting for our Twitter account. I tweet somewhat unconventionally—more from an angle of a personal account. Why? First, so I don't get bored. Second, so the audience doesn't get bored. As an added benefit, it's enabled me to avoid having to create a personal account. (I'm personally not all that interesting.) It also prevents me from crossing lines I might cross with a personal account (although I still probably cross a few lines with the business account).

I don't just tweet about the restaurant. There's really only so much I could say. I figure, our username tells you who we are, our website has our menu, and you can always read reviews about us online if you're deciding whether to visit us. Although I do post reminders about our menu offerings, my approach is to join right in with the masses and comment on music, pop culture, or just daily living. Honestly, it's more fun when I *don't* talk about the restaurant. I know when I scroll my Twitter feed, I like to see businesses tweet about events going on in their neighborhood, a cause they take interest in, or just abstract frivolity. It gives them a sense of humanity—something I can connect with as a person and a guest. It also softens the "eat here today!" read I'm already inundated with from everybody else.

> **NOTE**
>
> Some people think businesses shouldn't express opinions on social media platforms (or anywhere else), but I disagree. All businesses are run by human beings, and human beings have feelings, opinions, and value systems. (Maybe corporations really *are* people?) Has saying something someone doesn't like cost us business? Probably. But we will be ourselves and stand by issues we feel strongly about. In the end, it's our account, we can say what we want, and we're not forcing anyone to read it.

Chapter 9: Marketing

If you strike a good balance between fun and promotion, your number of followers will increase. And as you get more followers, they'll start to do your social media marketing work for you.

Don't Forget to Follow!

Social media is a two-way street. In other words, you can't just talk—you also have to listen. That means following others online. Honestly, I get more enjoyment by following others on Twitter than by being followed. I love keeping up with the saga of people's personal lives. Their expressions of thoughts, interests, loves, irritants, and setbacks are fascinating. Plus, if you are in the sales business—and if you open a restaurant, you are—you will find no better place to tap into the public's psychology in rapid-fire, easily digestible, bite-sized chunks than Twitter.

> **NOTE**
> I always find it funny when people say they're not really themselves online and "you don't know who I am." After all, even if you've created this fake, made-up persona, doesn't it still say something about who you *really* are?

I've been active on social media since 2009. I've noticed that since then, user content has gradually been stripped of any reservations. People are letting it all hang out. I see more tweets about food, sex, and racism than anything else in my timeline. I think it's a beautiful thing. What it tells me is we're comfortable enough to publicly share our innate obsessions with pussy, dick, food, and skin color—things that we have in common and also make us different. Maybe once everyone sees we're all just as weird or dysfunctional as the next person, real discussions can begin on how we can better understand one another, see things from a different angle, and hopefully get smarter as a species. Or maybe we're all just bored and have run out of other things to talk about.

> **TIP**
> You can do more than just follow people on social media—you can form connections that help grow your business. We've worked with commercial real estate brokers, accountants, and attorneys—all of whom we met through social media. We might never have intersected with these people if we hadn't found them on Twitter. Observing and interacting with them—reading their jokes, rants, or favorite songs—sped up an acquaintanceship that, while not made in real life, made us comfortable enough to seek them out professionally.

Dealing with Customers on Social Media

Social media is, well, social. That means there are the requisite "applause" and "boos."

Let's start with the applause. Whether you publicly acknowledge each and every compliment you receive is up to you. Lots of businesses retweet or repost any kudos directed their way for all their followers to see. That can be taken as humble pride by some or subtle narcissism by others, so it's only sort of a half-win for you. In my view, it's not necessary to respond to each and every mention you get online but it's nice to interact as much as you can.

That goes for negative mentions, too. And believe me, you'll get them. Mistakes big, small, and imagined happen all the time, and you can bet that—fair or not—somebody somewhere is bitching about one online. Sadly, the Internet is a major platform for keyboard thuggery, and there's not much you can do about that. The fact that an anonymous person can post a nasty message seen by thousands can leave you feeling like you're playing defense most of the time.

> **NOTE**
>
> What stumps me is that the people with the snidest comments never seem to have attempted to address the issue on site with the server, manager, or owner. Instead, they pull a guerilla warfare–style hit-and-run attack. But nine times out of 10, if the person would have just brought up their problem while still in my store, we could easily have resolved it to his or her satisfaction!

You have two options when you get a negative mention. One option is to ignore it—and that may be the way to go, especially if you feel like the claim is false, the situation was exaggerated, or the person behind the message is being a bully. The other option is to address it. After all, if you accept the applause while everyone's watching, you should be big enough to accept the boos, too. If you are active in your restaurant and know the place inside and out—as you should—you will be able to deftly respond to any service or kitchen missteps that get flagged on social media. Plus, being transparent rather than evasive can work in your favor with the broader public. Oh, and one time you should absolutely, positively engage online is if you're faced with an indefensible service issue, like the one we had with our cook who gave everyone in line the finger. A situation like that is worth smoothing over as quickly and as publicly as you can.

Chapter 9: Marketing

> **TIP**
> When dealing with customer complaints, handle it until its resolution in the original medium. That is, if it came via a tweet, stay on Twitter, etc. If, however, the situation is too convoluted or bizarre to resolve in a few sentences, then take it offline and handle it with a phone call. (Yes it's still OK to talk on the phone!)

I have read that because of social media, brands no longer have complete control over their message or image. In my opinion this is bullshit from marketing types preying on people's fear of criticism or apprehension about speaking for themselves in a tough situation. The truth is, you are *always* in control of your brand, no matter what is said, positively or negatively, about it! I've told people "no," disputed the accuracy of stories, and simply ignored the rants of weirdos from day one, and will continue to do so. If someone boycotts our establishment and "tells all their friends to do the same" because we won't be bullied or held hostage online, well, so be it. Such is the risk of the entrepreneur.

> **NOTE**
> There are always two sides to a story. If you or your staff were in the wrong, admit it. If you weren't, you don't owe anyone anything.

E-mail Marketing

For me, the jury's out with respect to e-mail marketing. Most people don't feel like opening the e-mails they already get, even for important stuff like their job, let alone your "meatballs from around the world" café and bistro. I have no problem with occasional e-mails from brands, but depending on the frequency, they can feel intrusive—at least to me. And if I'm really being honest about it, there's no restaurant, including my own, doing anything interesting enough for me to receive multiple e-mails a week from them. (There are exceptions, of course. If you're a retailer of some kind, like a butcher or fish market, then e-mail is a perfect way to announce new arrivals and specials, offer some background on the sourcing of your products, and even share tasty new recipes featuring those same products.)

The way I see it, social media is like the mall. If I go for a stroll through the mall, I expect to see promotions in my face from a business, so it doesn't bother me. E-mail, on the other hand, is a bit more personal. It's like my house. If I get too many messages in my inbox from a business, it feels like someone's knocking on my door at dinner time. So here's the deal: If I'm a fan, and I gave you my e-mail, I'm more than likely a regular, right? That means all I need is an *occasional* reminder of what's happening—maybe twice a month—and I'm good. Any more than that, and I start to feel like the Jehovah's Witnesses are in my neighborhood.

Guerilla Marketing

When we opened our restaurant, it was in a popular midtown neighborhood—an entertainment and arts district filled with local bars, family-owned restaurants, and retail shops, along with offices and galleries tucked away in 100-year-old buildings. We were a block off the main drag. Weekdays, the area was a veritable ghost town. It picked up on weeknights, and the weekend crowds were great. Nevertheless, we quickly learned that if we didn't draw a decent lunch crowd Monday through Thursday, we wouldn't be around too long.

"Aside from standing on the main drag and directing people to our shop," I thought, "how can we get people to come in?" The answer was simple: *Stand on the main drag and direct people to our shop*. We had a sign made with our logo, address, and an arrow printed on both sides and attached it to a wooden stick, like a picket sign. Then we offered a down-on-his-luck guy from the neighborhood $8 an hour to stand on a corner on the main drag for two or three hours every day at lunchtime. He needed the money, it was cheaper than a billboard, and it was the next best thing to having someone walk around with an old-school sandwich board on his shoulders. I even held the damned thing myself one Halloween while wearing a mask and chef coat. This "man on the street" approach worked well and offered a whimsical addition to our already-quirky part of town.

For a brief time, we offered delivery in our immediate neighborhood. Using a car didn't make sense, though, because parking outside our shop was always a problem. Instead, we bought a beachcomber-style bike and put a basket on the front. I'd load up orders and merrily bike through the neighborhood, making deliveries to hair salons, offices, and other small businesses. As I did, I'd ring the little bell we put on the handlebars and wave at passersby. Tips were good, and it was a great way to get to know people in the area. And of course, with every order, I left menus behind.

My point—and I do have one—is that this type of guerilla marketing works. So think creatively and have fun with your ideas. When it comes to marketing your spot, there are no rules!

Chapter 9: Marketing

> **TIP**
> An easy way to introduce yourself and your business is to reach out to schools, churches, and youth athletics groups in your area. Offer a special night for their organization, with a portion of sales going back to them.

Creating Value Through Scarcity

If you're opening on a shoestring budget, it's not the end of the world if you're forced to limit your days or hours of operation. In fact, you can use this to your advantage, creating value through scarcity—playing hard to get, if you will.

Honestly, places that do this intrigue me. They set parameters on when I can visit, and they don't care if it's convenient for me or not. If it's open only Thursday through Sunday, then that's when I need to catch them. Sure, it may be out of economic necessity, but I don't know that. As far as I know, it's their strategic way of protecting their brand.

> **NOTE**
> I'd much rather kick ass for four days out of the week than do "just OK" for six or seven anyway.

On a similar vein, if you were only able to swing an obscure, non-traditional, or hard-to-reach location, play that up, too. If you have a far-out concept that's worth seeking out, people will find you. Maybe you got a hell of a deal on an abandoned car wash or closed-down funeral home. Make that oddity your shtick! You're already half-crazy to be in this business, so you never know what might be a hit.

To Discount or Not to Discount?

This one's easy: Don't. Even if this is your first venture into professional foodservice, your brand should stand tall and mighty on its own, with no freebies or discounts such as BOGO (buy one, get one) or Internet coupon deals through third parties.

> **TIP**
> I'm not wild about discounts, but making your own frequent diner cards for a freebie after so many visits is never a bad idea. It's your place, and your call!

Hold your ground on your pricing and see how the market responds. If you're competitive or even a bit higher than your peers with similar concepts, most people will have no qualms about trying you out—and you won't leave precious income on the table, which you'll need early on. Personally, I'm the type who wants what he wants, when he wants it. I don't spend time scouring the Internet for deals or specials from my favorite places, and I don't mind paying full freight. If it's not in the budget to go out, get what I want, and leave a proper tip, I eat at home.

> **NOTE**
>
> Groupon and other similar outfits operate on a variation of a sales split with the owner, but for restaurants, I don't see the value. For one thing, what you net from the sale is barely above your food costs. Besides, most people who use these don't come back and pay full price. (They will tell you different because they're supposed to.) But it's your call. The same thing goes for radio and TV deals. With these, you get "free" advertising with the station in exchange for discounted coupons or gift cards, which their listeners or viewers buy from their website. Your call here as well.

Do You Need a Marketing Company?

Shortly after you open, you may find several "branding" or "marketing" people at your door, all offering their services to generate some buzz for your new place. They may be local or from out of town, and will typically offer packages that include social media and other promotional avenues, custom-tailored to fit your business. You can rest assured that none of these things will be cheap.

I have friends in this industry. At the risk of upsetting them, I will tell you (and they probably would, too) to approach some of these outfits with caution. Yes, there are formidable marketing and brand strategists who know what they're talking about. They offer straightforward solutions to problems without the flowery language and marketing buzzwords. Others, however, are 21st century snake-oil salesmen. These are the ones who can't coherently explain what realistic return on investment you should see. Think about it: Anyone can technically call himself or herself a "marketer." Starting a marketing firm isn't hard. And with today's "tech speak," it's easy to make the job sound a lot more complicated than it really is.

Chapter 9: Marketing

So how can you tell the good ones from the bad ones? Perhaps ask a few questions along these lines:

- What is your background?
- Have you been formally trained or educated in the field of marketing?
- Were you a product manager or marketing strategist for another company before starting your own company?
- Do you have any background in the foodservice industry?
- What can you do for me that I can't do for myself?
- Can you share some insight about people's buying habits as it relates to my business?
- Can you provide me with client testimonials? May I speak with them?

> **CAUTION**
>
> After the economic meltdown in 2008, when thousands of jobs went away, many people started their own businesses—ones that could be run from home without employees or licensure. This included a bevy of so-called marketing/social media/PR firms. A few figured out how to make money, the rest didn't. Their backgrounds varied. Some worked corporate jobs in varying capacities, others were from the failed mortgage industry, and still others were ex-finance or administrative people from car dealerships or homebuilders. There isn't necessarily anything wrong with that. Just make sure you properly vet an organization before committing any hard-earned dollars.

Don't get me wrong—I'm not telling you to avoid engaging a marketing or PR company, but I'm not here to shill for them either. There are probably 10 books coming out this week for marketing and salespeople (compared to one—if that—on how not to go broke in the restaurant business). So they have enough of a voice. My job is to save you money and focus on where your spending is going.

In the end, if you partner with a marketing company, it should be their goal to ensure you get the best leg up. To make sure that happens, be clear with your goals for your concept, give them what they need to help you, and expect to pay for their services. And remember: Although they can get bodies to your door, once those bodies walk in, the rest is up to you.

> **TIP**
>
> If you're interested in finding out how a marketing or PR firm can help you, do it sooner rather than later. Don't wait until you get into deep trouble with your business. It's harder to turn around a restaurant going down the tubes than you might think. At that point, you need a total overhaul—and for that, you need an actual restaurant consultant, not a marketing specialist.

Chapter 10

The Pop

You've opened your restaurant and survived the first few months, with all their hiccups and confusion. By now, you should be settling into a semblance of a routine.

Most likely, you will have gone through a few or even several personnel changes, both in the kitchen and up front. This is normal. You should have a few reviews (good or bad) on the Web, and you've gleaned what you could from them.

Because you took the time to plan ahead, and you didn't overspend and wind up opening too deep in the hole, you may even be pulling in enough to meet your monthly obligations to the business and maybe even at home. You're putting in the hours, and for the most part, each week is a little better than the last.

If the place hasn't burned down, and if you haven't ruined community relations by cursing at and throwing out dissatisfied guests, you will eventually get a sustained crush of patrons—what I call a *pop*. A pop is a day when, out of nowhere, all hell breaks loose and you are so busy it hurts. These days are painful, but necessary. They need to happen with you there, seeing it through from beginning to end. It's the only way you will feel in full control of your business.

Our Pop

With the burger joint, our pop happened on Labor Day of our first year. We had opened the previous April and had had a profitable summer, but we weren't setting the world on fire. We decided our first year to be open all holidays except Thanksgiving and Christmas. We found, however, we tended to overstaff on these days. So when Labor Day came around, we decided to have only two people on site: me and an employee named Matt. I gave Dario, our other cook, the day off because I didn't think we'd be too busy. The plan was that Matt—easily one of the best employees we've ever had, even to this day—would work the front and I'd stay in the kitchen, handling the cooking. We had worked like this before and made it through what we considered busy days with no issues, so there it was.

Things started off slow. The first two hours, maybe we served two people. Then, some onesies and twosies dropped in. Here and there, we got a call for carryout. At most, I dealt with five tickets at a time. No sweat. Then things changed. Out of nowhere, we looked up, and a line had formed from the register to the door. Soon, it snaked out the door and down the sidewalk. Then the phone started ringing off the hook. Matt kept up as best he could. As for me, I tried not to panic as the kitchen printer spat out one ticket after another: burgers, chicken, tuna—everything we had on the menu, all with special instructions for different burger temperatures, split tickets, extra crispy onion rings, sauce on the side, you name it. I got terribly behind—"in the weeds," as they say. I repeatedly called Dario, but he didn't answer. And Erin couldn't help—she was home with our two-year-old and four-year-old. Matt and I were on our own.

The only thing we could do to get through it was to get through it, so I turned my ball cap backward, took a deep breath, and hunkered down. First, though, we took the damn phone off the hook. At that point, carryout orders were out of the question. Then we dug in. I told him to be up front with everybody. When they got to the register to order, he warned them they were looking at serious wait times—maybe up to an hour. A lot of people got pissed and left. Those who stayed came to the counter every 10 minutes or so, grumbling and asking for their food, despite Matt's warnings. (I didn't understand this. They could see there were only two people working!) The 80-seat patio next door quickly filled up with people, and there was no end in sight.

I'll give it to Matt. He calmly held the down fort, smoothing things over as best he could. Me? Not so much. I got further and further behind. Eventually, I just let it all go. I got into the best groove I could, methodically working each ticket while trying to make as few mistakes as possible. I constantly wiped my face with my shirtsleeves—not just because of the sweat, but because of the tears. The combination of runaway joy from the crush of business and indescribable pain from my failure to capitalize on the opportunity was hard to handle at first. We were terribly unprepared, and I was so afraid of fucking everything up. Plus, I *really* had to pee.

Even as I sweated and cursed and, yes, cried, there was one thing I refused to compromise on: the order in front of me. These guests had already paid, and they deserved to get their food how they ordered it, hot from the fryer or off the grill. So I

Chapter 10: The Pop

took my time with each and every ticket. Besides, I knew if I screwed up—which I did, several times—I'd have to re-do the order, putting us even further behind.

Around 5 o'clock, Dario finally called me back. He'd seen all the missed calls, so when I answered the phone, he quipped dryly, "You busy?" I wanted to laugh, but I couldn't. Instead, I barked, "Man, where the fuck are you?!" He took my panic in stride. He knew I was really yelling at myself, not him. Hell, I was the one who'd told him to take the day off! He told me he was on his way home from out of town and he'd be at the restaurant within the hour. When he arrived, we didn't say much to each other. No explanation was needed. He took one look at the kitchen, which was in shambles, and at the bugged-out expression on my greasy, sweaty face, and knew what had gone down. He jumped on the line and started jamming right by my side. Together, we knocked out the orders, and eventually there was more metal than paper visible on the ticket holders. The feeling of relief—I can't describe it to you. It was like the first breath you take after being underwater too long. After half an hour, Matt and I took turns using the bathroom and smoking a cigarette. Then we headed back into the warzone, where the three of us banged it out until the 10 p.m. close.

As we washed the pans and mopped the floors, we shared a good laugh over the fact we pulled it off. Sure, we got yelled at and messed up some orders. But we *finished the day*. We also vowed from that day forward, we would be the ass kickers, not the ones getting our asses kicked. This was *our* house. Ultimately, the experience gave us *confidence*.

We'd have a similar pop the following spring, after a flattering article in the paper. It wasn't our busiest day, maybe 500–600 covers, and we were short on help that day, too, but we made it through. Our busiest day would come the next summer. That time, we were locked and loaded with enough staff and our prep game had been perfected. It was a Saturday, and all I can remember is we ended the night with 423 tickets, each with anywhere from two to five covers. Mind you, we were still in an 800-square-foot space, so it was hard, but those experiences prepared us for just about anything.

We learned to schedule enough people and allow for breaks—something important with a high-volume, quick-service concept. If it turns out you're not busy and need to send people home, so be it. But it's way easier for cashiers and cooks to make hours up than to try to operate with half the people you need. It will take you some time to figure out your minimum needs with respect to staffing. We were able to figure ours out only after being around long enough to review sales histories and to forecast volume.

> **TIP**
>
> Making payroll can be tough during the slow winter months, but it's well worth it to take care of your crew and let them keep as many hours as possible. That way, they'll be more likely to stick around for when you really need them in the spring and summer. The way I see it, we carry them in the winter, and they carry us in the summer.

Dealing with It

If you're running a catering operation, your pop might occur on a random afternoon. Suddenly, your phone will start ringing off the hook, and you'll find yourself awash in so many orders from new clients, you'll have to turn down a few bookings and readjust staffing and delivery strategies.

If you're running a restaurant, the pop may come from positive media exposure. Or, it could just be the result of the sun, stars, and moon aligning in your favor. Whatever the reason, it *will* happen. When it does, odds are you won't have enough staff or inventory, and your guests will cry bloody murder over their wait times. All you'll be able to do is get through it the best you can.

> **TIP**
>
> If you're in the middle of your pop and you've been caught short staffed, be proactive. Inform your guests of the obvious: There will be a wait. It's now on them to make the choice between leaving or staying and waiting their turn. If people decide to stick around, at the very least, make sure you get their order right. Oh—and it doesn't hurt to offer them a token of goodwill for waiting. A free drink or cookie is a small gesture, but goes a long way with most people.

When you're in the thick of it, and it's miserable, and you wish you were someplace else, just remember: *It has to happen for you to learn and improve.* So don't run from it. As the owner, you're the captain of the ship, and you need to face that pressure. If you stick around when the shit gets thick, you'll earn the respect of your crew. More than that, it builds strength to draw from as you continue your journey. Trust me: Once you get a few of these under your belt, you'll be well on your way.

Chapter 10: The Pop

Really, this is what separates the winners from the pretenders. The pretenders—if they're even on site—will go hide in their office, leaving the manager and staff to figure things out. The winners will be all over the damn place and loving it.

> **NOTE**
>
> As ugly as this day may be, embrace it. And when it's over, review what went wrong (and right) and figure out how to do things better, faster, and with fewer mistakes. From this day forward, a full dining room with a line down the block is exactly what you'll want to see—and you'll do nothing but grin at the beautiful chaos.

Chapter 11

Your Guests

After a few months, you'll notice your place is a little grungier than it used to be. This is good. You should *love* coming to work first thing in the morning to find cigarette butts and trash in the parking lot. You should also love seeing empty toilet paper rolls in the women's bathroom and piss-splashed men's room floors. Why? Because it means people were there! Cleaning this up should bring you joy because at least a mess was made for you to clean! An empty dining room is the loneliest place on Earth—and don't let anyone tell you otherwise.

You Are in the People Business

Opening a restaurant, you might think you're in the food business. It won't take long for you to realize you're actually in the *people* business. People are the key. The food will take care of itself.

So who are these people? Well, there's your staff, of course. No doubt, they're important. But even more critical are your customers, or as I like to call them, guests. You won't survive without them. They're the ones who will determine if your business lives or dies, so don't ever take them for granted!

Your guests will come from all walks of life, but the majority of them are just like you—people trying to get through life, who have a lot on their minds, and who, from time to time, want to treat themselves and their families to a meal away from home. They expect courteous service, a pleasant atmosphere, and good value for their money. When they visit, you must be thankful they've chosen your place. After all, they likely had literally hundreds of options, and it was your restaurant that came to mind.

In the early days of the burger joint, Erin and I were awestruck by the loyalty of our guests. Even if it was five below zero in the middle of January, these folks would park blocks away and walk to our store. There were times it felt like we were on the brink of going under when suddenly, we'd have a fantastic day or weekend, making everything just fine. It was as if angels had been sent through our door, always in the nick of time. We are forever grateful for those people!

If you're lucky enough to have these types of regulars, show them some love. Comp their orders every now and then. Give their kids a free dessert just to say thanks for keeping you in their rotation.

> **CAUTION**
>
> It's great to get to know your regulars—but it may not be the best idea to enter in any kind of business relationship with them. Sometimes it's just easier to deal with strangers. That way, if there's a falling out, everybody goes their own way, and you don't lose a valuable guest. When we had issues of non-performance with people we'd met through the restaurant, we got hit with "You know how much of a break I gave you on that job?" or "As much as I come in your place, you're really making this big of a deal about it?" So I suppose a half-assed job is the tradeoff for them coming in the restaurant now and then.

Understanding Who's Who

I enjoy observing people when I'm out around town—what they're doing and what they're buying. I like to classify them as shift workers. Each shift has its own mode and personality. As a foodservice operator, you'll serve, shop, and be in the general vicinity with some, or all, of these shifts.

The first shift consists of people out and about between the hours of 9 a.m. to 5 p.m. (or 7 a.m. to 3 p.m., or what have you). This shift mainly includes homemakers, retirees, and the unemployed. Your retail shopping experiences at this time of day aren't crowded with the bodies usually present in the evenings or weekends. There's a calmness to this crowd. They're not in a big hurry. Often, they're very budget-conscious. You get the most objective viewpoint on what's moving in stores and what's popular when it comes to dining choices as they're careful with their spending and looking for a good deal. Ask yourself: How can you capture that segment for your concept? How should you market to them? If you can win them over, turning them into regulars, they'll supply the precious weekday business that keeps you afloat.

Chapter 11: Your Guests

Second shifters are a bit different. These are the people out between 4 p.m. and midnight. They may be first shifters who are off work, students who wrapped up their classes for the day, or again, the unemployed. Often, they're in more of a rush. If they're coming home from work, they're usually taking kids to practice, picking up dry cleaning, stopping at the bank, and trying to figure out what's for dinner. If they're students, they're getting errands done before doing homework, working a part-time job, or hanging out with friends. Because this shift is juggling so much in such a short time, they tend to be more spontaneous. They make quick decisions and don't overthink things. How could your business serve them best? Would a streamlined delivery or carry-out system for this crowd be a profitable niche? If you're a corporate breakfast and lunch caterer, would it make sense to market a home meal delivery on weeknights? You could add big numbers to your bottom line by working just two or three hours in the evening.

The third-shift—midnight to 8 a.m.—crowd is the most interesting to me. They can be any age or sex and include second-shifters leaving their jobs, blue-collar workers, the party crowd, other entrepreneurs such as yourself, and sadly, again, the unemployed. You'll mingle with musicians and other creatives at this time of night, as well as enjoy the lively company of the city's biggest pimps, whores, drug-dealers, and gangsters. Like first-shifters, these people are rarely in a hurry. Third-shifters don't take any shit while they're moving through the dark streets of the city, but they're some of the most considerate people around. Third-shift folks will push your car out of the snow and help you if you lock your keys in the car. Car battery dead in the lonely 24-hour store parking lot? Third-shift dude *keeps* cables in his car and doesn't mind giving you a jump. I was at a store in the middle of the night and came up short on cash after everything was rung up. The third-shift lady behind me went into her purse and fronted me the $2 I needed so I could get my ass moving and, better still, *she* could be on her way. If you're open 24 hours, you'll cater to these third-shifters. How will you capture their attention? Have fun hanging out with the third shift and observe what they're spending money on.

> **NOTE**
> Third shift is also a quiet time for you, the operator. When we catered, this was my favorite time to shop at the grocery store because the place was always empty. It's also a great time to scout locations for your concepts in a calm and uninterrupted manner.

The Good, the Bad, and the Ugly

Most guests are wonderful people. Truly. But unfortunately, not all of them are. If this is your first go-round in the business, you must be aware of how the public can *really* be. (And I'm not talking about critics here—we'll get into them later.)

At my restaurant, I and my staff have been yelled at, cursed out, and worse. We've had people throw fits in the dining room. We've had people steal from our dining room. We've had people purposely make messes, just because they can. People come in drunk. People come in smelling bad. People come in looking for a fight, for no apparent reason. People come in and shoot dope in our restrooms.

Speaking of restrooms, one morning, I got to work early and was greeted with a turd in the men's room urinal. Not the end of the world, but still, I thought, "Why would someone do that?" The toilet was right next to the urinal! But that was the least perplexing aspect. The gross part was the shit ball was just that—perfectly formed, about the size of a golf ball. I wasn't mad as much as spooked. What sick bastard would take the time to craft a perfect sphere of shit and just leave it there? At some point, you have to wonder who in the fuck raised these people.

> **NOTE**
>
> As frustrating as this episode was, the co-conspirator was our own staff, who obviously failed to do a walkthrough at closing the night before. Or, they did, and chose to have the morning crew deal with it. To this day I half expect to walk into the bathroom and find someone passed out or OD'd on the toilet.

No doubt, you will experience bizarre and unruly behavior. When it happens, you must take a stand. Be firm on what you will not tolerate and have rules in place. If you have a dress code, enforce it. If you have to tell someone to leave and never come back, do it. If you need to call the police, call them. Yes, your business is open to the public, but it's still private property. That means you are not obligated to serve anyone who chooses to act a damn fool. This is about your survival. It's about all the hard work and money you've invested. So fuck them and the $20 they "won't spend here anymore."

> **NOTE**
>
> As it is with the people you hire, put any stereotypes out of your mind. The people who exhibit this bad behavior come in all shapes, sizes, and colors.

Chapter 11: Your Guests

Scammers and Hustlers

The first day in our new location was a busy one. At one point, a guest called in to complain that we'd forgotten the onion rings for her carry-out order. Given how chaotic things were, this seemed plausible. The cashier who answered the phone told her to come in and we'd be happy to give them to her. She seemed satisfied with that, and we went back to work.

Not five minutes later, she called back and, in full tirade mode, said she had another problem. I took a break from the kitchen to personally take the call. I calmly asked her what happened, and she lit into me. "There was gum—a piece of *green gum*—in my chili cheese fries!" she shouted. "I want my damn money back. And I'm still coming for those onion rings!" I listened to everything she said. Then I asked her if I could please call her back so I could check on some things.

I dug through the receipts and tickets until I found her order. She had indeed ordered and paid for both items, so that was legit. But I knew something she didn't. "Yep," I said. "Just as I thought." I took a deep breath and called her back. When she picked up the phone, I introduced myself as the owner of the restaurant and I thanked her for coming in. I told her that we'd be happy to give her the onion rings—I couldn't prove we hadn't forgotten them. Then I said, "As for the chili cheese fries, no go." I continued, "And I don't ever want to see you in here again." She screamed and shouted and ballyhooed. "I worked in customer service," she yelled, "and I would never come back to your store, after the way you've treated me!" She continued, "Oh, and you can bet I'll be calling the health department. I'll have you shut down!" Blah blah blah. I let her go on for a while, and finally told her "Ma'am I made your order myself. No one is chewing gum in our kitchen, so don't try that shit here." Still, she did come in for the "missing" onion rings. When she did, I handed them to her myself. "Thank you for visiting," I said politely. She snatched the bag, turned on her heels, and left.

There are people who feed their households with these hustles. We've had someone call a *week* after a supposed error was made on our part and demand their entire order be comped. Another person claimed he ordered six burgers "the other day" and three were missing the *burger*. They got a bun with lettuce, tomato, and onion, but no meat. What kind of dumb ass hustle is that?

When I encounter this type of nonsense, my first course of action to get as much information on the transaction as possible—what time they came in, what they ordered, and what method of payment they used. I tell them with this info, we can go back into the point-of-sale system, find and reprint any tickets and receipts, and then get to the heart of the matter. Usually, I find the longer I'm on the phone and the more I probe, the weaker their stories get.

You won't just encounter free-food scams. You'll also find yourself dealing with donation scams. Someone will come in complete with official-looking paperwork, tri-fold brochures, and a clipboard and ask for a (cash) donation for some type of youth outreach activity. Then there are the contractors—the ones who say they've gotten an OK from the landlord to patch the roof or parking lot. All they need is $250 from you, which the landlord will reimburse. Rest assured they'll know the landlord's name and maybe even have his phone number—which they will have called just before entering your shop to make sure it's going to voicemail. Then they'll stand there confidently as you call the number to verify the story. We tell these people to keep it moving.

Dealing with Actual Charitable Requests

Five minutes after you open, you'll start getting requests for donations. Although it's always good business to support good works in the community, whom you choose to support (or not) is totally up to you. You simply can't afford to give to every cause that comes across your desk. You must use your common sense about how much and how often to give.

If you think making a donation will help your bottom line, if it's something you feel morally obligated to do, or if it satisfies a commitment your business has made to give back whenever possible, then do it. Conversely, if it doesn't make sense financially or is incongruent with your personal morals or values, you are well within your rights to decline. You should also feel free to decline if you don't have the resources, the organization or individual seems sketchy, or the requestor is rude or pushy.

When your business opens, you may not be able to give much at all. That's OK. Your focus should be getting on your feet. When you're in a position to start donating, by all means go for it. There are many things you can do to help out your community. At our place, we've mentored high-school kids, hired ex-cons, donated to food rescue organizations, fed hungry people who have come in short of (or with no) money, and donated thousands of dollars' worth of gift cards. We've always felt that the more we give, the more we get back—and you will too.

Chapter 11: Your Guests

> However we've set up some rules with respect to donations. First, all requests must be made via e-mail or business letter. No walk-ins, phone calls, or social media platforms. If applicable, 501c3 information should be included. Second, we set a quarterly budget for donations and do not waver from it. We respond to all solicitations for donations on a first-come, first-served basis. If we deplete our first-quarter budget in mid-February, so be it. We won't donate another dime until April 1. And second, we rotate contributions. That way, we have a chance to partner with as many organizations as possible.
>
> When impolitely confronted with a request we can't honor, I explain our decision like so: "We can no more donate to every request we receive than we can expect you to visit our restaurant each time you are hungry." Still, I've found myself in public squabbles on social media for declining to donate to causes. One time, an individual with a large social media following called us out for just this reason. He posted how we weren't "about the community" or some such bullshit. His followers, after hearing only one side of the story, then flooded our timeline with an array of "fuck you" and "I'll never visit your restaurant" type messages. I'm talking dozens of them. These, I gleefully retweeted for all our followers and anyone else watching, mainly to show we gave zero fucks. Unfortunately for the requestor, we had reached our charity threshold and had nothing left to give. It didn't matter who it was. (In the end, after some discussion about the timing of his request and an explanation of our procedure, we were able to patch things up with this person, who is indeed very generous in our community.)

Miscreants, Knaves, and Ne'er-Do-Wells

Recently, I was talking with an industry veteran. In the mid-1980s, he and his partners had a quick-service restaurant in Union Station, a 19th century train station in downtown Indianapolis that had been beautifully restored in the hopes it would become a showpiece destination. There were several restaurants, nightclubs, and even an attached hotel. This guy opened one of the first businesses in the food court upstairs and the reception was phenomenal. Sales averaged $6,500 a day (Mind you, this was in the 1980s). But within a year, business dropped off and for the most part died—not just for him, but for everyone in the food court.

"What happened?" I asked him.

"In part," he explained, "because of the ne'er-do-wells."

Ne'er-do-wells come in all flavors—and can have a terrible effect on your operation. Typically, he explained, they would arrive around 10 p.m., about when the nightclub opened. Too young to get in, they would loiter in the food court—taking up tables, ogling women, and spending no money. There wasn't crime or violence *per se*, but enough people became uncomfortable they stopped coming to the food court altogether—hence the precipitous drop in this guy's business.

The problem, they realized, was these mostly young people had nowhere else to go. To address this, he and the other shop owners proposed a solution to the property manager: Brick over the narrow, alley-like streets outside the building and close them to traffic at night. Create a pedestrian mall, so to speak. Maybe install some nice gas lamps and wrought-iron furniture and invite some food vendors in. That way, anyone who was too young (or too broke) to get into the clubs upstairs could hang around outside and be IPD's problem. Then create one main entrance where IDs can be checked and dress codes enforced. The entire top floor could even be 21 and over if they wanted. It never happened.

I understood his frustration. Our own neighborhood went through the unfortunate events that occur with unruly denizens. Oddly, in our case, it was in part a product of the area's success. Being attractive for its small, packed bars and restaurants, most proprietors did quite well. The streets were full every weekend and owners of the real estate enjoyed escalating rents and property values. Naturally, entrepreneurial types—seeing the prosperity in the nightlife—opened more of these places. The problem was, the number of places quickly outgrew the population to support them. Plus, each spot wasn't all that different from the next. So how did they try to get bodies inside? They lowered the prices. And if one lowers its prices, then everybody has to lower their prices. This led to a situation where there were too many places competing too cheaply for too few patrons. This attracted an element that otherwise wouldn't have had the area on its radar, which led to an increase in crime. Not surprisingly, several businesses left the area, and those that remained had the unenviable task of hiring extra security and having to more or less selectively admit patrons into their bars and nightclubs. Since then, things have vastly improved. But what happened was a common enough evolution—a quaint village evolving into a city neighborhood and everything that comes with it. You can't really fault the landlords or tell an operator they can't pursue their dream. So it is what it is.

As an owner what can you do if you see this coming? Let's say you've spent more than $100K to get your business off the ground. Should you let it be ruined by a few bad

Chapter 11: Your Guests

apples? No! You band together, put together some ideas, and hope everyone works for the greater good of maintaining an attractive atmosphere for people from all walks of life to enjoy. And if everybody stays on the same page, hopefully it works. You also stick to the rules you set for your business, which I talked about earlier. The bad element rarely lasts once the community decides it's time to deal with problem straight up without worrying about hurt feelings or being labeled as anything other than a concerned citizen.

Chapter 12

Handling Criticism

A person might have an idea for a restaurant, a plan for opening it, and even the money to get it off the ground. Yet, that person never makes his or her dream a reality. Why? For many, it's simply the fear of criticism.

No one wants to experience public failure or embarrassment. Sure, you remember that game-saving play you made, but chances are that memory holds less sway in your mind than the time you tripped and fell in the cafeteria, were publicly rejected by your high-school crush, or were fired from your job. The inevitable feelings of inadequacy and hurt can cast clouds of self-doubt, stripping away the confidence you need to take the necessary risks to lead the life you really want.

Traveling the path of a foodservice operator means being willing to accept a litany of critiques, put-downs, and rejections—with the bonus of having invested thousands of dollars for the privilege of receiving them. And yes, it hurts! After all, your restaurant is a reflection of *you*. Your menu consists of food *you* like. Your place looks like it does because that's how *you* want it. Essentially, when you open a restaurant, you're saying to the public "This is who I am and what I like. I want to share it with you." If the public shares your vision, you might keep your doors open. If not, well, you'll just have to figure out why not and try again. Either way, don't take any of it personally.

> **NOTE**
>
> The more you know your business, the better you'll deal with people talking bad about your baby. Change things up where obviously needed, and stand your ground when warranted. After a while, you'll be able separate which areas genuinely need improvement and let go of complaints from people bitching about nothing.

Niche-Based Criticism

Your business's niche can play a big part in how it is received by the public. Here are a few points to keep in mind:

- If you decide to open a restaurant featuring regional or ethnic cuisine but either your restaurant isn't located in that region or you don't belong to that ethnic group, expect to be held to a higher standard. Be ready for swipes about how you've missed the mark and aren't staying true.
- You'll likely get a break if your menu reflects an ethnic group of which you're a member. In general, being from a different part of the world and serving native dishes will give you wider latitude with the public. But even then, you'll be subject to criticism for failing to prepare a dish the way someone else might. In this case, no one is really right or wrong, so as an owner, you want to sell your guests on why you do things "your way."
- Those of you taking a straightforward American approach will have much less wiggle room. Everybody has their opinion of what the quintessential burger joint, steakhouse, or diner should be.
- Be careful about advertising with that tired expression of "such and such 'with a twist.'" Most of the time, said twist is undetectable. Even if you do manage to put a twist on something, let the public make that proclamation. Just do what you do and take the credit for being creative.
- Speaking of being creative, note that it is not the same as being weird. What we've seen in the burger segment has ranged from the truly clever to the shockingly desperate, with combinations that, for lack of a better word, are nauseating to contemplate. (Of course, if the operator sells them by the thousands, what I think of them doesn't mean jack shit. But you follow my point.)
- If you're entering a crowded segment and are more or less offering a "me-too" concept—think coffee, sandwiches, burgers, BBQ, etc.—be prepared to defend your value proposition, why you are different, and why people should spend their money at your restaurant.

The "Write Stuff"

There will be three different people with something to say about your concept, each with their own following and sphere of influence:

Chapter 12: Handling Criticism

- The food writer
- The restaurant critic
- The Internet reviewer

Food Writers

In my view, the food writer is the most laid back and objective of the group. This person may do a restaurant review from time to time, but typically delves deeper into the industry. He or she might cover business issues in foodservice, food history, and profiles of the local culinary scene, as well as share recipes and announcements of restaurant comings and goings.

Restaurant Critics

This person writes with a focus on the overall experience at a restaurant and the delivery of its product to the guest. The restaurant critic informs his or her audience of the quality, presentation, service, and atmosphere of an establishment, with either a recommendation to visit or areas needed for improvement—hopefully done with some flair and a well-rounded perspective. To be as objective as possible, this person typically visits a restaurant multiple times before committing a review to print. I don't think restaurant critics are mean-spirited or look to make life difficult for operators, but they can be very unflattering if your place doesn't have its shit together.

The first time our restaurant was reviewed by a critic for a local paper, we'd been informed in advance. We even knew what day the critic's group was coming in to the shop. "Slam dunk!" I thought.

The day they arrived, I was much more nervous than I thought I'd be. Even though we weren't terribly busy, I found myself scrambling around the kitchen, trying to get their order perfect, all the while aggravating the cooks with my bullshit and worry. From time to time, I peeked out from the pass to see how things were going. Overall they seemed to be enjoying their food, and after about an hour, they left.

When the review came out a few weeks later, I grabbed a copy of the paper and rifled through the pages to find our write-up. I was certain it would talk up our cool new place and tasty vittles. After all, our customers had said nothing but nice things, and business was steadily going up. I figured the review would give us a helpful push. Plus, we'd have something to frame and hang on the wall.

The air in my little balloon was quickly let out. The review was incredibly average, with comments about under-ripe tomatoes on the salad and a burger that was too dry. The fries got decent treatment, and I think we got points for creating a nice atmosphere in a small space. But beyond that, it wasn't clear if they were all that interested in coming back. Needless to say I was bummed. It was our first legit review before an audience of thousands, we'd had the benefit of knowing they were coming, and I wasn't even *thinking* about displaying that thing on the wall.

As I read the review a second time, I ran their visit through my mind. I replayed everything as clearly and as objectively as I could. In the end, I had no choice but to be completely honest with myself: They were absolutely right about everything. During my rush of seeking perfection, that burger *was* probably left on the broiler a little too long. And obviously, neither the staff nor I had checked what shape the salads were in before they went out. I had been so frantic, not wanting to make any mistakes, I ignored simple quality-check measures we'd had in place for weeks and wound up being forgetful about things that should've been a no-brainer.

Internet Reviewers

These include bloggers, review site rock stars, and random guests. Some are anonymous and some aren't. With it being the Internet, many think they're smarter and wittier than they actually are. These folks can cause some angst for operators because of their drive-by tactics. Sometimes they'll pen an entire treatise of their opinion on the projected success or failure of a new concept based on a single visit.

> **NOTE**
>
> My biggest issue with Internet reviewers is they'll complain about a problem at a restaurant but never mention whether it was brought to the attention of the staff. I don't know of any operator who wouldn't correct a problem for a guest, but these cut-and-run reviewers don't speak up. Instead, they cast the staff as clueless dumbasses who can't run the place properly. Unfortunately, this "keyboard courage" has eroded our ability to talk to each other to resolve conflicts—and it's not going away anytime soon.

One Internet blogger guy wanted us to feed him and his girlfriend for free in exchange for a review on his site. I politely declined, basically telling him we'd take our chances, and that even if people were going to write about us, we wanted to get paid. He continued to press the issue, going on about how much it would help our business. I guess he was saying he was "semi-famous" in the local media community. I actually

Chapter 12: Handling Criticism

thought he was joking throughout, but he wasn't. Fortunately, he finally went away. The whole thing was just lame.

We don't write reviews. Being operators ourselves, we tend to cut restaurants some slack when we go out to eat. We can usually laugh at their mistakes because we've made the exact same ones. We've learned from experience that one night you can be firing on all cylinders and the next you blow an engine. People don't show up to work, equipment breaks down, or the cooks are out of sorts. It happens.

Responding To (or Ignoring) Critics

Look, you're human and your place is run by humans. Everyone makes mistakes. Occasionally, your paying guests will be the victim of these mistakes, they'll write about them, and it will sting. All you can do is own up to your legitimate *faux pas*, correct them, and move on. That's all you owe to anyone. After a while, you'll be able to filter the negative comments that may come your way and determine whether their actionable or not.

> **NOTE**
> The cleanliness of your shop should never come into question. After all, that's something you can control. Service, on the other hand, can go any number of directions, because it's a product of the people—the highly fallible people—who deliver it. Your best defense here is to hire well, get buy-in from your team on the goals and values of your operation, and have someone with some sense in charge in your absence at all times.

Should you pay attention to what's being said about you? Of course you should—up to a point. When you read reviews about how overrated your restaurant is, your food is average and uninspiring, your menu is lacking in creativity, your prices are too high, or your attempt at regional cuisine is a complete failure, you should take them to heart if and only if your sales are weak. In that case, the reviews may well be accurate, and you have some work to do. If your sales are strong, however, then you shouldn't give a fuck about any jabs thrown your way, barring those that pertain to service missteps or a gross error in technical execution. If a guest has an issue and it's our fault, I care, and I do everything I can to make it right. If people simply prefer a competitor's style over ours, who the hell am I to judge their taste buds? As for complaints from guests about our prices, I tell them, "I understand. They should be higher."

> **NOTE**
>
> You'll definitely want to pay closer attention to reviews when you're first starting out. It's one way of getting a read on how you're doing. But after you've been around for a while, you can quit reading them so religiously. By the time you're, say, three years in, and your numbers have continued to go up, you can pretty much assume the public has voted and you'll be around as long as you want to be. With our own business, we're fully aware of our strengths and weaknesses, so we don't get too wound up. We just try to keep improving.

As for whether you should respond to a review on the Internet, my answer is, it depends. If the reviewer wouldn't recommend your place because he or she didn't like your food, I wouldn't worry about responding. Just be happy the person came in and tried your place out. If business is steady, then you have nothing to worry about; obviously, plenty of people out there like what you do. Remember, your place isn't for everybody, and that's OK.

If, on the other hand, there was some issue with the service provided by your staff, a response might be in order. First, however, I would get my staff's and any witnesses' side of the story. Once, we were called out on social media for being "rude." The person demanded an apology. But when I asked for specific examples of how we were rude, the person couldn't give any. I knew Erin had been the cashier on the day in question, so I asked her if she remembered any hiccups with this individual. It turned out that what got the guest upset was the fact that my wife didn't remember who she was—an honest mistake, considering the thousands of people we come across in our line of work. In the end, I didn't give the woman an apology because we didn't do anything wrong. Sometimes people just need to get over themselves.

In the event of a real failure—if someone has a legitimate beef—it's perfectly OK to own up to it and apologize, even if the guest is extra nasty with their words. Don't linger too long on it, though. Just take the hit and move on. Fix the problem and stay on the offensive for holes in your program. It's also OK to chime in if someone is spreading misinformation about your business. After all, you've made a serious investment with maybe hundreds of thousands of dollars at risk, not to mention the jobs you've created and any goodwill you've earned in your community. You should have no reservations about defending yourself. Just pick your battles wisely. Oh, and begin *any* response with a thank you to the person for coming in to your place, because they didn't have to choose you that day.

Chapter 12: Handling Criticism

> **NOTE**
> A popular local restaurant made the news a while back for conspicuously posting a statement asking guests to inform staff of any issues with their visit so they may be corrected before jumping on the Internet and talking shit. (I'm paraphrasing.) The reaction to this approach seemed to be mixed. Some people felt it's not the restaurant's place to tell a guest how to complain; others said they're simply trying to protect their brand with a common sense suggestion. I don't have an opinion either way, but I think it's impossible to stop someone who prefers an Internet beat-down to a personal conversation.

I wouldn't stress to the point of removing negative reviews and I certainly wouldn't pay a service to do it. If you're doing your best to offer quality food and good service, let the chips fall where they may. Besides, every paying guest has a right to his or her say.

Enjoy the good reviews and learn from the bad ones. Don't fret too much over people who knock your fabulous creation down a few notches from time to time. If you're still open and making money, then you obviously know what's going on. No need to lose sleep. Just be humble and thankful for anybody who walks in your door. They easily could have gone someplace else.

> **NOTE**
> Just having balls enough to open your own business puts you in a different category than 90% of the people who have an opinion of what you're doing. Don't let them rattle you. If you believe in yourself and your ideas, you will be able to counterattack those little voices in your brain that tempt you to doubt your decisions after an unkind word or two is said about your place.

If your shop experiences a slip in ratings or rankings, even if you feel things have been pretty consistent, this is a wonderful thing! It tells you that you're getting more visits and therefore more opinions. You got the visit, which was the victory. Everything after that was based on the subjectivity of the person choosing to share the experience. Hopefully, the majority of experiences are good ones, but as time goes on and more and more people visit your place, the chances of dissatisfaction also increase. Think of it this way: Would you rather have an approval rating of 95% based on 100 visits or 85% based on 1,200 visits?

Hey! Our Place Was on TV!

Your place was on TV! Nice! Now what?

Anytime you get any sort of exposure, national or otherwise, first thank the food gods. Then prepare yourself for a surge in business. It goes without saying your numbers will go through the roof, at least for a time. Be ready to handle the extra load in the kitchen. Give the staff a pep talk about keeping up their great service and keeping the place in tip-top shape. It's everybody's time to shine!

Remember, now that you're on the map as a destination, people will have certain expectations (fair or not) when they visit. Remember, too, that you just never know who will come in. Maybe it will be your next franchisee or big investor. Maybe it will be a quality individual who wants to work for you and be part of your brand. Above all, don't take it for granted.

This kind of exposure can work against you in the hands of a persnickety guest, however. A few years ago, the family and I were in Manhattan and stumbled into a bakery. We'd never heard of the place—it was just another stop on our Saturday afternoon stroll. It was busy, but it didn't strike me as anything more than a typical New York bakery in the middle of summer—until I damn near knocked over an easel with a gigantic poster proclaiming that the bakery had been featured on so-and-so's food/travel show and THEY WANTED US TO KNOW ABOUT IT, DAMMIT. Clearly, based on what I could tell was tourist traffic, they seemed to be enjoying a nice bump as a result. But just like you, me, and everyone else they weren't perfect. The floors looked like they hadn't been swept since that morning, the staff was curt and inattentive, and nearly half of our bag of goodies should have been removed from the case a day earlier. Was any of this a big deal and would I write about it on the Internet? Fuck no! The place more or less met our expectations—a busy Manhattan bakery being run by mostly young people who'd rather be someplace else on a Saturday afternoon. But I see how a fan of the TV program who made special plans to visit could have made a five-paragraph issue of it online.

Regardless of how well you respond to the bump in business, the honeymoon will eventually end. This is a fact of life. Enjoy the fame when you get your turn, but treat every day after like the day that got you noticed in the first place.

Chapter 13

The People in Your World

In addition to your employees and guests there are several other people who are crucial to keeping your business running smoothly. These include:

- Delivery drivers
- Repair technicians
- Accountants, attorneys, and other professionals

You'll also find yourself in close quarters with your neighbors. For insight into dealing with all these different players, read on.

Delivery Drivers

Think about the people who deliver your product. These guys bust their ass. All day and night, they're climbing in and out of trucks, pushing dolly after dolly of boxes, sorting and lifting thousands of pounds, climbing up and down flights of stairs. That's their routine. They work *hard*.

Introduce yourself to these people. Get their names. They may be a bit brusque—they'll likely keep it moving as they talk—but you'll find they're decent, hardworking people, just like you. Offer them a soda or sandwich every now and then to show you appreciate their hard work and hustle, and they'll remember your place as a "good stop" and look out for you when they can. Maybe they'll move your drop up a few places on their route, making your day go easier. Or maybe they'll relay some information ahead of an official company announcement, giving you time to make adjustments. And they're always up on openings, closings, and bits of local restaurant gossip.

In addition to treating your delivery people like human beings, the other key to a great relationship with them is to thoroughly communicate your terms and expectations. For example, if you can't accept deliveries between 11 a.m. and 1 p.m. because it's lunchtime, say so. We had an issue with a driver who consistently unloaded everything at our back door around 12:30, at the height of our lunch business, and then snuck off, figuring it was close enough to our scheduled drop-off time of 1 o'clock. Then he started leaving it earlier and earlier, to the point that one day, he dropped it off at 11:30. We were slammed until 1 o'clock, so it just sat outside at the back door. Fed up, we called the vendor and refused the shipment. We weren't accepting delivery on product left sitting outside for an hour and a half! The driver had to come back, reload the entire order, and take it away. We ordered sporadically from them after that, and eventually stopped doing business with them altogether.

Another delivery person pulled an even bigger blunder. At our first burger joint, we had an old, non-working, 8×10–foot walk-in cooler behind our building, which we used as a storage shed. We ran power to it and stuck a chest freezer in there to keep ice cream and other items we didn't have space for inside. One hot July afternoon, Matt went outside to discover the ice-cream delivery—12 three-gallon tubs—had been set next to, but not inside, the chest freezer, where it was *supposed* to be. All that was left was a puddle of sticky, fly-infested goo that took an hour to wash away. Matt did the best he could, but it being the middle of summer, he couldn't get everything. The baby-shit stink it left behind lingered for weeks.

Even if your place has an awkward access, storage, or stairs situation, you need to tell your delivery person to place your order exactly where it needs to go, not where they feel like putting it. When we moved to our new location, a new bread delivery guy balked at the basement stairs he'd have truck our bread racks down. He gave a long sigh with a "Well…I dunno…I've got a bad back…." I looked at him and shrugged my shoulders and nonchalantly told him that's where the bread goes, and I certainly wasn't going to be the one who put it there.

> **NOTE**
>
> Some suppliers offer "key drop" delivery service for those clients who spend at a certain threshold. In other words, you give them a key along with the alarm code, and they'll deliver your order in the wee hours while you're closed. The upside is, your order is delivered and can be inventoried first thing in the morning, before things get hectic. The downside is, no one's there to check for errors or quality-control issues. We used key-drop briefly but stopped. I prefer to be physically present for deliveries don't like have too many keys to our place out on the street.

Chapter 13: The People in Your World

Get to know your delivery drivers and treat them respectfully. But remember: *You* are the customer. Make sure you clearly articulate your procedures and expectations, and you'll enjoy a smooth relationship with your delivery people and the vendors who employ them.

Repair Technicians

I promise you: Things will break down in your restaurant—always on your busiest days or during the weekend. Fortunately, should you get into a jam, there are repair people out there who can fix anything…for a price. We've spent thousands of dollars fixing shit that breaks. It's the *worst*. From $2,000 for motors to $200 repairs on sandwich prep tables, we've watched money that should have gone to our bottom line go right out our door. It's going to happen, so be ready.

It's a good idea to have a list of these people at the ready *before* things go wrong. As mentioned, I strongly suggest you compile this list before your grand opening. At the minimum, you'll want to have techs on hand for the following:

- Equipment and hood
- IT/POS system
- HVAC
- Electrical
- Plumbing, sewer, and drain
- Exhaust hood
- Locksmith

These people repair what can severely interrupt or even halt your sales during business hours.

> **TIP**
>
> Develop a rapport with your repair people. These folks will save your ass. Be friendly when they show up, even if you are losing your mind. Pay their bill on time. And shop around like you would for any other supplier.

Larger service and repair companies will be more expensive, but may be the best bet in the long run. They have an actual address and staff, typically offer a guarantee, and can usually get to you the quickest, even at odd hours. In contrast, an independent repair person or, as some call them, an "alley mechanic," will generally save you money. However, this person may or may not arrive in a timely manner. Or, he or she might abandon you in the middle of a job. This person may also fall out of contact, move, or abruptly quit or retire, leaving you without any follow-up on a job that needs revisiting. In other words, with these people, there are limited guarantees. After a while, you'll find a good mixture of companies and solo technicians and know who to use for what jobs. We have been through many repair people over the years and found the best approach is dealing with an established company while still having a few independent operators on deck.

> **TIP**
>
> Network with your peers to find out what companies and solo operations they've had success with—and always share the good ones you find as well.

In addition to the technicians mentioned, you'll also need to keep on hand contact info for the following:

- **Dishwasher repair:** Assuming your broadline supplier provided you with a dishwasher, you should already have a service agreement worked out for this.
- **Fountain drink machine repair:** Whatever company you've partnered with for your fountain drinks includes on-call service. It's a good idea to conspicuously post their repair hotline on the rack where you keep the syrups.
- **Ice machine repair:** We lease our ice machine, an arrangement that covers all service calls and reimbursement for any bags of ice we have to buy while the unit is down.

> **The $6,000 Lesson**
>
> Six weeks after we moved the burger joint, we needed to have the exhaust hood cleaned. Although we didn't have any major issues with our regular service people, we decided to give a new company a shot if for no other reason than to have a backup. These companies work overnight, when restaurants are closed for the evening. I let the techs in around 10 p.m. and asked them to call me when they were finished so I could come check the job and then lock up for the night. They called me when they were done, around 3 a.m., and I headed over to the restaurant. I was happy to discover that the place was spotless. The stainless steel hood and backsplash gleamed. They made a great first impression. I thanked the techs, signed off on the work order, and went home.

Chapter 13: The People in Your World

When I got back to the restaurant a few hours later, the prep cooks were working on the line, but something wasn't right. Thick smoke from the grills and fryers hung in the air. We stopped the prep, shut off all the equipment, and propped open all the doors to air the place out. It turned out that the hood, while running, had no suction.

I immediately called the cleaning company and told them about the situation. "No problem," they said. The guys were still out in the field and would swing by in about an hour. I began to worry, though, because we were opening in less than two hours and only half the prep was done. When they showed up, I held a piece of paper up under the hood. It should have instantly stuck to the filters, thanks to the air uptake from the fan on the roof. Instead, the paper floated gently down, disappearing behind the char broiler. We looked at each other. "Yep," one of them said. "Not workin'." No shit.

As a backup, I called a friend who owns a mechanical company and asked him to send somebody out. He came out himself, along with his tech. The five of us climbed up on the roof to inspect the fan. When we did, we discovered what looked like grenade shrapnel. It appeared as if someone used a pair of pliers to bend back portions of the ring inside the fan assembly.

The cleaning guys didn't admit to anything. They said all they did was open the fan and use a high-pressure hose and some degreaser to clean the fan blades and other inner workings. The rest of us thought this story was bullshit because it had been working fine not 12 hours earlier. It was our consensus that when they were cleaning, they fucked up the balance of the blades somehow, which were probably scraping against the inner ring of the unit, and used a pair of pliers to try to correct the problem. The only real solution was to replace the fan. Fortunately, my mechanical guy was able to find one locally. He got his crew on the job and everything was up and running by the end of the evening. Still, I'd had to close for the day and send my crew home, and of course we lost a whole day's worth of business.

Throughout the morning, I called the owner of the cleaning company to talk about what happened, to no avail. After a few hours, their operations manager finally called me back. After I explained the situation, he told me in so many words they weren't responsible for any damage done while cleaning. Unmoved, I sent an e-mail to the owner detailing what had happened. It went unanswered, as did every other message and call I placed over the next month.

It became clear they had no plans to work with us, so I decided to take the matter to small claims court. Mind you, we are not lawsuit people. But I figured, hey, they decided to make a business decision, so we'll make one, too. All told, we were out about $6,000 once you added up lost sales and the purchase and installation of a new fan, so that's what we asked for.

After about a year, our case was finally called. The cleaning company never said they damaged the fan and never said they didn't. Their defense was the work order I signed that night after I got back to the restaurant. The fine print at the bottom of the page held them harmless from any damage to equipment they clean. To make a long story short, there was case law on both sides, we won in small claims, they won on appeal, and we walked away with nothing but legal fees.

Morally did they owe us? Sure, I think so. Maybe not $6,000, but we felt they owed us *something*. Legally, however, they didn't owe us shit—at least, that's what the judge ruled on their appeal. We had no choice but to take the L and move on. Would it have been good business for the owner of the cleaning company to throw us a bone instead of dragging out a three-year court case? Of course. But he figured we'd never do business with them again anyway, so why bother? Better to take his chances in court. And that's how it went down. (And this is why America is in the shapes it's in.)

The takeaway here is to clearly understand the liability of any companies that work on your equipment, especially something than can cease your operation—potentially for days. Ask for and—this is important—*actually read* all work orders and agreements beforehand. And of course, don't sign off on anything until you're certain everything works as it did previously. Scrawling my name in a hurry to get home cost us big time. Would we have won the case if I had never signed that paper?

Attorneys, Accountants, and Other Professionals

With the previous story in mind, I'll tell you that it's wise to have an attorney. (Hopefully, you'll only need them to put together money-*making* deals for you!) You may at some point need the services of real estate, contract, or tax specialists. Again, ask around to find out who has experience with good ones. Oh, and get your checkbook ready.

Chapter 13: The People in Your World

If your operation is small and you have the patience, there is plenty of software out available for you to handle your own bookkeeping. Still, it's not a bad idea to hire a bookkeeper or even a CPA. A bookkeeper, who is typically very affordable, offers an extra set of eyes, can help you stay on top of any tax changes, and generate financial statements. That frees you up to focus on running your business. If your needs are more complex, then a CPA may be the way to go. A CPA provides the most comprehensive service, handling any complicated tax filings associated with your business while staying on top of any new rules or regulations. As with everything, shop around until you find the right person. Not every bookkeeper or CPA is created equal. If you don't like the one you hired, find someone else. We've changed a few times.

> **TIP**
> Keep clean books for the banks and any possible investors or buyers you may have down the road—or if not for them, you damn well better for the tax man.

You obtained workman's comp and business insurance before you opened, but when you get a breather, shop your insurance around. We've had fluctuations of as much as $1,000 between policies. Know what your coverage is and make sure you have enough.

Neighbors

Unless your establishment is the only building as far as the eye can see, expect to deal with neighbors. Unfortunately, we've witnessed or experienced strained and eventually soured relations with commercial and residential neighbors in every location we've ever been in. It always came down to one thing: the age-old battle over real estate.

To start things off on the right foot, make it a point to meet as many neighbors as you can before you open. Inform them of your plans and that you're happy to be joining their community. You want to make friends early because eventually, the honeymoon will end. This is especially true if you generate more traffic than they expected. In that case, be prepared for squabbles from time to time over trucks blocking driveways, trash blowing in their area, or your people parking in their spaces.

If your neighbors consist of other businesses rather than residents, don't be surprised by a minor (or major) shakedown. The neighbor, seeing all those extra bodies in your place, may ask you to sign a lease for a portion of their property to accommodate your customers who want to park, stand, or sit there. In fairness, they have a right to, and you'll need to decide what this is worth to you. On the one hand, you can't physically police where every single one of your guests parks or sits down, and ultimately it's the responsibility of said neighbor to enforce the rules on his or her property. On the other hand, if you wind up with lines out the door and hour-long wait times, you really may need the extra space for your guests. In that case, it may not be such a bad idea to sign some sort of an agreement with your neighbor. That would ensure your guests don't have any hassles when they visit. In this scenario, you win, your guests win, and the neighbor wins.

Remember, though: The neighbor can *ask* you for rent, but cannot *force* you to pay it, their tow trucks be damned. If you do your due diligence and post signs noting where people can park and sit, then the public can read for themselves and assume their own risk. In that case, you can tell the neighbor you're not paying them shit—although you'll want to phrase it more professionally.

Either way, pick your poison. If you can negotiate a deal that's fair for both sides, it may be worth the extra expense. If the neighbor insists on a figure you feel is outrageous or you financially can't handle, then let the public work it out with the neighbor. Maybe there's a middle ground to be had, maybe there isn't. Still, you must press on.

Interview with James Jones, Chef/Restaurant Owner of His Place Eatery in Indianapolis, IN

Why did you get into restaurant business?

I never intended to get into the restaurant business. It was sort of a progression. I didn't even start cooking until I was probably in my late 20s. My mom had a small catering business and I started helping her with that. I liked it and really got into the creative side of cooking. She eventually got tired of it and I wound up doing it on my own. Now at the time, I was working full time in radio advertising. Later I decided that one day I wanted to go to culinary school and learn more about food. My very first class was a food theory class. The chef that taught the class said that for every single class, we were going to have a project, and if we picked one concept or one idea that we liked and we stuck with that through every single class and project, by the time we finished we would have a complete business plan. It made me start to think about if I *did* own a restaurant, what would it be? My idea was an upscale soul food restaurant. By the time I was done, I had a full-scale business plan. Unfortunately I was going part-time, and it took me about four and half years to go through culinary school.

Chapter 13: The People in Your World

How did your restaurant eventually come together?

Some clients of mine from the radio station, some ministers, opened His Place Eatery. It was originally a soup kitchen that they flipped into a restaurant to raise money to continue to feed the community with the soup kitchen. They had no experience running a restaurant and closed after three months. They knew I had an interest in having a restaurant, so after they closed, they contacted me and asked if I was interested in buying their equipment. I got to talking with my wife and we said, why not approach them about buying the whole restaurant? But at the time, I didn't have the resources to buy it. A couple weeks went by and a buddy called me and asked me, "Hey, when are you gonna open that restaurant?" I told him I didn't have the money to do it. He said get a number from them and let's do it. After some back and forth, we went back and said, "Can you do this amount? We'll do the rest on payments over a two-year period." And they were like, "OK." And that's literally how we got started. By now, they'd been closed six months. After getting staff, cleaning the place up, and putting everything together, we opened 45 days later. We kept the name the same because after going through a laundry list of names we wanted to call it, it always came back to "His Place."

What has surprised you the most since you've been in the business?

One of the things I tell people all the time is if I had known how much work it was going to take to be in the restaurant business, I would have never done it. I came from wearing a shirt and tie. I used to tell people I was allergic to labor, and I end up doing one of the most laborious jobs in the world. You're lugging 50 pounds of potatoes; you're on your feet for God knows how many hours a day. And it does not stop. That was a huge surprise. Another one of the biggest surprises—and one of the most humbling things about it—is that people actually come in to eat your food. Whenever I think about that—my wife and I talk about it often—it's very humbling. It's like, wow.

Sometimes I wonder why we're still around. It is very humbling.

Yeah. They actually come in to buy what I have! And it all started from an idea, and the way I wanted to do things, and people come in and enjoy it and appreciate it. They recommend it other people. It's a lot of work, but it's really awesome that people come and pay their hard-earned money to enjoy it and walk away satisfied. Sometimes we talk about it and it just gives me chills.

Tell me about when you really started jumping off. What was your busiest day and how did you get through it?

In the restaurant business, busy days are all relative to the next busiest day. When we look back on what used to be the busiest days in the beginning, now we could sleep through those days. But I remember when we first started out—my background is marketing, right?—we decided to do an e-mail blast to friends and family to invite them to a grand opening and ask them to tell all their friends and family about our soft opening. A full meal and a drink for $6 or $7. It was on a Saturday, at a certain time—

A Saturday?

It was a Saturday. We had opened our doors for the first time on Friday. The e-mail went out earlier that week to get momentum for people to show up because we wanted feedback. So Saturday comes and the day starts off pretty slow. Then, when it got close to the time we put on that e-mail, all of a sudden people started coming out of the woodwork. We were jam packed. There wasn't a seat in the house. And we had no idea what we were doing. This was only the second day we were open. We had no real systems in place for when we got busy.

Did you have a kitchen printer?

At that time, everything was paper. We didn't have a POS at the time. Everything was written on the ticket. We didn't even have a system for carry-out or an in-house ticket. So tickets went back to the kitchen—

Ouch. Did you have enough people in the kitchen?

Yeah, we had about four people. We just didn't know what we were doing. I think we had a two-hour wait. I remember looking at all those tickets thinking, "Oh my God, what have we done? And how do we get out of this?"

One order at a time...

That's what I started telling people. Whenever you get overwhelmed, just take it one at a time. If you try to process too much, it's going to paralyze you. Pretty soon, you'll get a rhythm, and you can go from one at a time to two or three at a time.

Chapter 13: The People in Your World

We both started before social media was real big. Tell me about your experiences with that.

It's a necessary evil. I don't think there was anything back then that's even comparable to right now. When you made a mistake, it was almost private. It was between you and whoever you made the mistake with and the people they could physically talk to. Opening a restaurant in this environment, where social media is such a prevalent part of what we do, it's very, very intimidating and it's very difficult. Like the story I just told you, with all those people and all the social media accounts we would have been clobbered with—it could have been devastating to our business. I feel sorry for people dealing with that now.

You have to realize, social media has nothing to do with what we're doing and has everything to do with the person who's posting it. Social media is a "me first" thing. We're at a place where anybody can have a voice. We're all unknown until we post something on a social media site, so you have a lot of people patting themselves on the back thinking their voice is louder than what it is. And the way some people get power behind that is posting negative reviews. Customers are not always right. However, I do believe the customer should leave with some level of satisfaction, and I take that into the review process. If I respond to something, it's for the readers. It's so people reading those reviews know we care enough to respond to it to let them know we are aware of a mistake or something they didn't like. For the person who did the posting, that usually doesn't do anything for them because they're already on to the next thing. I've left my phone number on every review response I've ever done and I've gotten one call in almost seven years. It's not about correcting a problem. It's about them having a voice to blast off and say that there *was* a problem.

Besides having enough money, any warnings you'd give new people starting out?

I think one of the biggest mistakes people make when they get into the restaurant business is—and I tell people this all the time—there's the restaurant, and then there's the restaurant business. The restaurant—that's what customers come into every day. They don't want to know you're running a restaurant business. But you're running a restaurant business! What I mean by that is, when that person gets that plate, you need to know how much it costs. You need to know what's on that plate and how much every single item on that plate costs coming in and going out. If you don't know or aren't close, you have a real problem. I mean no disrespect to any large-scale chain restaurants because honestly, my goal is to be one of those someday. However, you've never heard anyone say, for example, "Hey, let's go to Applebee's because the food is outstanding!" No. They go because it's consistent. As local restaurants, that's one of the things we should strive to be: good, consistent restaurants that have a solid business. Places like Applebee's have a solid business, so you see them all over the place. If you were to talk to the ownership or an executive of Applebee's and ask them how much cost is in this chicken-wing basket, they're going to tell you *exactly* how much cost is in it. You need to do it the same way. You need to know where your rent, food, lights, and labor costs are. You need to be so on top of it that when it starts to get out of whack, you can immediately respond. There will come a time when you're going to be slower, and when you slow down, if you're not making a profit, it *will* show up very quickly. You're going to have to make *drastic* changes.

If you weren't in the restaurant business, what would you be doing? An entrepreneur with something else? Or a nice job with steady income?

Yeah, I go back and forth on this. I like to use sports analogies. Owning your own business is sort of like how the center always wants to be the point guard and the point guard always wants to be the center. You know what I'm saying? You love being an entrepreneur, but the workload and the volatility and emotional ups and downs—sometimes I'm like, man, I should have just stayed in radio. Even though radio is also inconsistent, at least I had my weekends, and at 5:30 I was at home with the family, you know? And I got up at a reasonable time. When you own a business, there were years that passed us by because we were so wrapped up in the restaurant. At one point, my wife and I went downtown and didn't realize they had all these new places down there. We were like, wow, we're like tourists in our own town! There's so much we haven't been able to experience because our nights and weekends are taken up. But even with those things there, I would still probably be an entrepreneur. Because I'll *always* be an entrepreneur.

Chapter 14

The Lifestyle

At our core, the people in this business are gamblers. Were into a twisted yet delightful form of self-punishment. If you don't believe me, just take a look at our lifestyle.

First, the Bad News....

Starting your own restaurant is a *lot* of work. There are long hours for weeks, months, or even years on end. There are boxes to be lifted, there is shopping to be done, and food to be cooked. It goes without saying you should have a formidable constitution for this profession. On top of that, between staff, suppliers, and others, there are easily 20 new people in your life—all of whom will have a direct impact on the function of your operation. .

Things will be especially difficult when you first start out. I've mentioned this a few times already, but I'll really drive it home here: You have no business being away from your baby—your newborn—at any time for at least the first year after you open. You must personally receive every compliment, hear every complaint, deal with every employee or customer meltdown, face every financial hardship, make every decision and resolution, and learn every lesson. You need to be on the scene for all of this, every day, counting weekends and holidays, for all four seasons. Whenever your place is open, *you must be there*.

> **NOTE**
> If you eventually want to be able to step away and enjoy a solvent operation, leaving you time to move on to other projects, travel, or enjoy good old-fashioned leisure time, you *must* make these sacrifices up front.

Some of you are saying, "But that's what I'm paying a manager for!" Well, yes, that's true. And if you're lucky and find a good one, that person will indeed make your life a little easier. But the fact is, *you* are the one paying the equipment repairman. *You* are the one who must make payroll. *You* are the one with your name on the lease. *You* are the one assuming all the risk. Your manager has no such worries. If you close shop, everybody moves on to new jobs at other restaurants, but *you* will be left to pick up the pieces.

> **NOTE**
>
> This is why I'm skeptical of those "save my restaurant" shows. These places have managers—sometimes more than one—as well as an owner who spends at least *some* time in the place. You mean to tell me nobody takes a stroll through the kitchen in the morning and notices how filthy it is? Some also claim they once were the "hot spot" in town. But if these owners were smart enough to make it work the first time, they had to be smart enough to notice when things started tanking, didn't they? Are they not looking at financial statements every month? My guess is when things turned, they *did* know about it—they just chose to ignore it. The owner decided to hide, at which point the manager stopped caring. Everybody else stuck around for a check.

Now, the Good News!

"Mark!" you're saying. "You sound like a kill-joy. I know it'll be hard work, but I got into this business to make money and have a little fun, too!" My job here, dear reader, is to share with you the truth. Of course it's fun. I don't know of any other entrepreneurs who have as much fun as we do. That's why everybody wants a restaurant.

One day, I was standing outside with the chef from the restaurant next door. We were chatting about the business and its eccentricities. He summed it up plainly: "If"—he paused for emphasis—"and I mean *only* if you have your shit together, it's like going to party every night." He was right.

The most interesting people you'll meet will be in and around restaurants. People from all walks of life are there for the same thing: a good time. It's awesome to be in a business that's about relaxation, socializing, and to a certain degree entertainment. We *are* the party. It's even better when you're making money doing it. I can't think of anything that compares to the rush you experience being a member of this group.

Chapter 14: The Lifestyle

> **NOTE**
> That rush is only compounded by the fact that there's an undercurrent of risk. Losing it all is very much a possibility, and for some people, that's part of the fun. The restaurant entrepreneur is the gambler at the craps table placing $100K on six and eight.

Setting Boundaries

Restaurants are sexy businesses. Real estate and bond trading are not. After all, what are bars and restaurants if not dimly lit, den-like rooms with music, booze, and human bodies in close proximity? No doubt, you've been to plenty of concepts with a sexy vibe. And whatever you can imagine people do behind the privacy of four walls is going on in restaurants. I'm not judging it, just stating facts.

Do bartenders and servers regularly chip in on eight-balls before work? Sure. In some cases, the bartender is the one *selling* the eight-ball. (When I lived in Manhattan, I was told risky trips to Washington Heights were unnecessary, as the best cocaine on the island was to be found in select bars around Wall Street.) Are after-hours sex parties fueled by top-shelf liquor and high-powered drugs occurring in the dining rooms of swanky restaurants? Of course there are. Does a restaurant convert to a private club on Sunday afternoons, with members enjoying high-stakes poker and drinks and served by scantily clad hostesses? Why shouldn't it? Do owners develop drug addictions, become alcoholics, and get into money trouble with unsavory characters? Don't be naïve. Is this bacchanalia a part of what you're signing up for? Not at all. Can an owner avoid this, keeping family and friends intact while running a successful business with a feeling of pride? Damn right they can.

Still, as the owner of your establishment, you might find the temptations that arise difficult to resist. It's up to you to set and enforce boundaries. For example, if you serve alcohol and drink alcohol, you must practice moderation. Hanging out at the bar before, during, and after service can be fun, but remember, the drinks are your product, so it is unwise to buy your friends drinks every night as you glide about the dining room. Along similar lines, your staff is also your product. It is therefore a bad idea to start fucking any of your employees. (Besides, they are already fucking each other and don't need your meddling.) If you must, fuck the restaurant people down the street.

With workdays ending late at night after an hours-on-end adrenaline rush, it's easy to overdo it. After all, there's always a good time to be had and a fun crowd available to hang out with. Make sure you respect your limits. People enjoy reading about the wild lives of chefs, servers, and bartenders. I do, too. But the difference between you and them is they are employees. They can fuck off as much as they please because they know there is *always* work in the kitchen. When the party ends, it's the owner who will be left with the bills, lawsuits, and bad credit.

Cars, Clothes, and Money

Being allowed to expense gas and maintenance for a company vehicle is just one of the many, many perks of owning your own business. Although you certainly can use your vehicle as a form of advertising, covering it with graphics and your company logo, you don't have to. Common sense says if you *do* decide to emblazon your brand all over your ride, you (or whoever else drives it) should stay out of strip-club or adult–toy store parking lots. I don't care where you go, but a potential customer might. You should also drive with a greater level of courtesy. That means not flipping people the bird, laying on the horn, or yelling "Asshole!" or "Bitch!" at fellow motorists. Whoever is behind the wheel is representing your brand.

Another perk is that you are now free to dress casually if you so choose. I promise you: You won't miss having dry-cleaning bills! As an added bonus, there is an expense category for "uniforms." For me, it consisted of a particular brand of hospital scrub pants rather than the usual chef's pants. In addition to a back pocket and two regular front pockets, these pants also have two additional pockets—one on each thigh—handy for storing a phone or small notebook. The pant itself is a very thin cotton material, so it's not as effective at protecting against hot grease or water splashes, but I like the airflow. There's nothing worse for a guy than your nut sack fused to your inner thigh from standing at a hot grill for 10 hours.

> **TIP**
>
> Some people dig wearing chef coats. If you have a sightline kitchen where guests can see all the action, then chef coats give a crisp, polished look. Your linen service company can supply you with fresh coats every week, and they're usually very affordable. Same deal with aprons.

If you don't do much cooking, then jeans or slacks with a logoed polo shirt is a great casual look. For a more laid-back approach, branded T-shirts with your logo on the front or back work just fine. You can also offer them up for sale to your guests. I also highly recommend a non-skid kitchen shoe.

Chapter 14: The Lifestyle

> **NOTE**
>
> When I was catering, I often made deliveries to the same medical offices I had called on as a sales rep for Megapharm not three months earlier. It made me chuckle how I was instantly unrecognizable in jeans and a polo pushing a lunch cart. The irony was that while working at Megapharm, although I wore suits every day and *appeared* prosperous, I was always broke by the third week of the month. The predictability of a steady paycheck made me much more lax with money. In contrast, the entrepreneur's lifestyle, with its irregular income, forces financial discipline and put me in the best financial shape I'd ever been in my life. Any credit-card debt was paid off within 30 days, my vehicle was paid for, and since I controlled my whereabouts, I could jump on a plane to Vegas or New York on a random Tuesday just because. As an entrepreneur you will *love* owning your own time.

Say you've been open a couple three years now. You're profitable. There's finally something left over at the end of each month. And of course, you are reinvesting in your business. There's an exercise I'd like you to do: Go out and buy yourself a treat—something you've had your eye on. The rule is, it has to be a tangible good—no exotic trip or plastic surgery. A car or a motorcycle works best. Set a limit of, say, $30K for something new or used. Do it now, while it's still relatively early, to purge that natural human desire for personal reward. No matter how trite it may seem, buying a toy or trinket with money you legitimately earned will satiate your hunger for that feeling of accomplishment. It will reinforce the idea there was a prize for all your hard work.

> **NOTE**
>
> Now, you have no business cruising around town in a Lexus if you still owe your brother-in-law $10,000. But if you've made it out of the woods, you've paid everybody back, and things are stable, there is nothing wrong with enjoying the fruits of your labor.

After you buy whatever you've decided on—a car, a motorcycle, or what have you—I want you to enjoy it for a year. Then I want you to sell it. Why? What this exercise will do is wire your mind to remember that obtaining things is very doable, and can always be done again if you choose. It will also teach you that sometimes, you'll have to let things go—and that's doable, too. Spoiling yourself by buying something and then letting it go will give you clarity about what's really important. In time, you'll see that in flush times and in lean times, all that stuff is just…*stuff*. (Also, the reason it should be something tangible is it gives you something to sell in the event you need cash.)

In my case, when things were going well with our catering business, I bought a particular German luxury car. I'd longed for one since I was a teenager. Now that I was in a position to finally drive one, I felt it was something I deserved. It was fun being able to shop for a nicer car, which for the first time I'd be able to pay cash for and drive away. I wound up finding one on eBay from a dealer in Texas. After a friend who lived there checked it out and gave it the OK, I wired the money to the dealer, and it was delivered around the corner from my house. Soon, however, the car lost its luster. It felt silly driving such an ostentatious car to the store for a pack of cigarettes. I usually wore kitchen clothes, so I always felt underdressed in it. And truth be told, after a winter of slipping and sliding on Indianapolis's streets and a spring spent swerving around potholes, I grew bored with it. Nine months after I bought it, I sold it. The cash came in handy when our daughter was born, enabling Erin to take the maximum six-month maternity leave allowed by her employer.

I did finally get to own a car I'd always dreamed of, but if I never do it again, it's no big deal. In my case, the materialism goblin had been fed and put to bed. These days, I drive a 15-year-old pickup truck and a 10-year-old minivan. And instead of rewarding ourselves with things, we do it with time.

> **TIP**
> If you've toiled for months or years in your business, don't hesitate to do something nice yourself. When you're able to enjoy yourself, be sure you do it. The opportunity may not come around again for a while!

Paying Yourself

You can pay yourself a salary, draw whatever is left over as net income from your P&L statement, or both. Regardless of what route you choose, at some point, you'll size up exactly how much money your store is making juxtaposed to your time and effort spent in it and decide how you wish to proceed.

Eventually, you'll want the freedom to work *on* your business, not *in* your business (unless of course your plan is to be present most days as the face of your brand). For

Chapter 14: The Lifestyle

example, suppose your cash flow is $110,000, but you're on the premises seven days a week, 12 hours a day. Is that something you want to keep up for the long term? Would $80,000 be enough if you only worked Monday through Friday from 7 a.m. until 4 p.m.? Or maybe you keep $60,000, but other than picking up mail and holding staff meetings, never work in your restaurant again? The less work you do, the more you'll pay other people to do it for you. The more work you do, the more money you'll keep. Somewhere in there will be your sweet spot in terms of freedom of movement and a reasonable income.

Monopoly Money and Honeycomb Hideouts

Not unlike artists during the Renaissance, who depended on patrons to underwrite them, the restaurant industry has its own clan of venture capitalists, devotees, wealthy hobbyists, and groupies. Like those artists of yore, foodservice operators are creative, have a passion for what they do, but have little or no money. Sometimes, they manage to intersect with well-heeled supporters who believe in their talent or idea and agree to support their vision. These relationships are formed every day and in many cases are necessary to even keep a culinary scene going. Closures announced and new opportunities on deck are hot topics for discussion and analysis. It's all fascinating to watch, really.

Those who've worked hard enough, are lucky enough, or are connected enough have the privilege of playing with what I call *Monopoly money*—that is, money in ample supply that, if handled right, will involve the same amount of personal risk as the money in the board game. Honestly, I can't think of anything better than to have other people's money build your playground. This is a major feat showing you're held in a certain regard and there are people willing to take a risk on your behalf.

Sadly Monopoly money is rarely available to the new or inexperienced. For the lucky few, however, it does exist. My guess is you need only a few things:

- Demonstrable talent with a track record and some type of following or fan base.
- An incredible ability to convince people to invest with you in one of the most statistically doomed segments in American business.
- Unwavering self-confidence.

Now, before you declare yourself a foodservice pimp or conclude you can win over the shrewdest investor with your charm and a few "best of" awards, consider these points:

- People with earned wealth aren't stupid.
- If others invest in your business, you may have creative control, but the business doesn't fully belong to you. You could be fired from the restaurant, even if it has your name on it.
- Your batting average should at least be .500, in my opinion. I'd invest with you if you opened four or five places and half of them are still around and profitable. For most people, those are pretty good odds in this business.

Although Erin and I have come close, we've never partnered with Monopoly money. Still, many others do. It appears if you've been around awhile, and say the right things to the right people, it raises your stock as a go-to operator who's a good risk in the eyes of people who enjoy being in the restaurant business. There are plenty of bullshitters and time-wasters, but money *is* out there, and everyone's looking for fresh ideas. Just be sure to give it your all when you get a chance so you get invited back to play.

> **NOTE**
>
> Can't play with Monopoly money? Don't worry. There will always be people with more than you, but everyone operates at different levels and with the associated headaches. Still, each level enriches the landscape. Wherever you play, be confident and keep doing whatever makes you *you*. Arrogance won't get you far, but it's OK to have a little swagger. This business is tough. If you're going to survive, you need to genuinely believe you're the baddest motherfucker in the room.

Monopoly money is the open faucet supplied by the wealthy and well-connected to the foodservice hustler with an idea, a track record, and the gift of gab. They've earned the right to license themselves. Their backgrounds may or may not be similar to yours, but they're foodservice people at heart, and contribute to the greater good.

There's another group of people who operate from a different perspective. These are the architects of what I call Honeycomb Hideouts. Remember those Saturday morning commercials from years ago for Honeycomb cereal? A group of neighborhood kids would gather at the Honeycomb Hideout in someone's backyard for adventures, laughs, and a bowl of cereal. The Honeycomb Hideout was a place to get away from the world and hang out.

I use *Honeycomb Hideout* to describe a different kind of hangout: one that's owned by someone who has lots of money, loves bars and restaurants, and wants to open one of

Chapter 14: The Lifestyle

his or her own—despite having no experience in the industry. The owners—who can be anywhere from their 20s to their 50s and hail from a variety of backgrounds—usually aren't concerned with critical acclaim or even profitability. Rather, the purpose of their venture is to serve as a clubhouse for drinks, food, and getting laid. Naturally, these people have no interest in working in hot kitchens, on the floor, or behind the bar. They hire chefs, servers, and bartenders to do all that. They aren't interested in partnerships, either. They have plenty of cash and don't *need* partners. And of course, some don't feel they need advice. They figure, they've made money somewhere else, so they must be smart enough to operate a restaurant. Not surprisingly, these establishments often lose lots and lots of money.

> **NOTE**
>
> Do professional athletes open nightclubs because they need the money? Does a group of wealthy 50-something men really care what kind of deep-fryer or stove to buy? I know I wouldn't.

There are Honeycomb Hideouts in every city, big and small. A Honeycomb Hideout can be something as simple as a dive bar with a short-order kitchen to a full-blown fine-dining establishment with marble bathrooms. Often, in the case of the latter, the owners will have spared no expense on the buildout. Some Honeycomb Hideouts are by design, while others are failed attempts at a legitimate operation and have morphed into Honeycomb Hideouts.

> **TIP**
>
> Not sure how to spot a Honeycomb Hideout? I promise you, after just a short time in this business, you'll be able walk into any concept large or small and, after staying an hour, on their busiest day, guess their weekly sales within a few thousand bucks. If you're in an establishment whose sales clearly can't support the business, you're in a Honeycomb Hideout. These places can lose money like no other.

Whatever you do, don't try to keep up with the Honeycomb Hideouts. Their resources will far outlast yours. And while I celebrate and support these places, I will respectfully ask some of their owners to have a seat if I hear any chest-pounding about business acumen. If a business is on life support with regular cash infusions from any source other than its customers, it is *not working*. I don't care how cute it is or how famous the owners are. The math is the math.

Restaurant Winners

The problem with some Honeycomb Hideouts is they're often owned by people who aren't serious about the business. As a result, there may be half-assed service, sub-par food, and inconsistent operating hours—none of which will ingratiate them with the public. Gaining the public's trust is no small feat, as any full-time operator can tell you. Competing with restaurants and bars ambivalent to the struggle can make it even more difficult—a problem only compounded when the Honeycomb Hideout closes, sending a poorly trained staff back out into the industry and vexing an already hard-to-win public.

Maybe one day, you want a Honeycomb Hideout of your own. I'd like one myself. And believe me, there are more of them out there than people realize. Your best bet is the usual strategy: Buy one that's failing (or has already failed) and already has all the bells and whistles. You can then inexpensively redesign it to suit your needs, enjoy a good run of playtime, and, since you saved on a buildout, maybe make a few bucks while you're at it.

If you're in the Honeycomb Hideout club, be the best friend you can be to the industry. Run a tight ship like you would any other business. Take it seriously enough to respect the people working for you who may really need that job. If you get bored, don't ignore it, sell it.

Monopoly money players and Honeycomb Hideouts peacefully co-exist in the landscape with hardscrabble operators. In fact, to have any type of variety in a city's restaurant scene, they need to be there. The margins in a restaurant are such that it would take *years* to open other units or concepts solely from their profits. Fresh money has to come from somewhere. Let the players play. And hell, maybe you'll work together one day.

Chapter 15

Things Fall Apart (The Lifestyle, Part II)

Here's a quick story on how to go broke when everything's going right. Not long after our most profitable year, Erin and I faced the biggest challenge we had ever worked through. We had an investment opportunity we were sure would pay off in about 12 to 18 months. After all, the previous year's financials with our little burger joint were strong. Even if they went down a bit, we figured we'd still be able to cover all our bases. It would be tight, but doable. We could not have been more wrong!

For many of us in non-touristy cold-weather climates, the peak money-making months are March through June. We typically experience a pull-back in July and August followed by an uptick in September. October through December is usually pretty good, but January and February are killers, with business down by 40% or more. The usual strategy is to sock away cash during the flush spring and summer months so we can tap it for payroll, inventory, higher gas bills, etc., when we're starving in the winter. If there's not enough cash set aside, we'll get by with credit cards or lines of credit, which we pay off when things turn around in the spring. Our investment would consume the majority of our cash reserves and all of our available credit. Although our accountants advised against it, saying the math didn't support what we were trying to do, being hard-headed people, we were convinced we could make it work. After all, our sales were up! What followed was the roughest financial period of our adult lives.

Due to a perfect storm of a downturn in sales at the restaurant and our investment revealing many hidden flaws, we were financially crippled by the end of summer. By the time winter came around, we had no cash and had maxed out all our credit. We were forced to take about 40 hours from the front- and back-of-house staff and work them ourselves to stretch as much incoming cash as we could. Still, we barely made payroll. Vendor invoices went unpaid. Eventually, we got so far behind they took away our credit, forcing us into involuntary COD status. We had to pay our sales taxes late, incurring penalties. Our company van blew a rod but there was no money to fix it. I let it sit and did all the shopping from my pickup truck, stuffing cases of lettuce and 25-pound bags of onions inside the tiny cab on days when it rained or snowed. All we could do was pray none of our essential equipment broke down, as there was no money to repair or replace anything.

Of course, the public wasn't aware of any of this. To the outside world, nothing appeared out of order. We never skimped on the quality of the inventory we purchased. But if anyone had walked into the cooler or pantry, they wouldn't have seen much of it in there. The lights and gas were still on; no one had to know we were two months behind on the bills.

To put it bluntly, we were in the shit. We ate at home most of that year, pilfering inventory from the restaurant to make dinner. Things were far worse than when we had both been laid off. Now, we had people we were responsible for, we had a lease on a building, we had a $1,000 electric bill each month for said building, we had no credit to tap, and we owed everybody in town. Being in-between houses, we couldn't borrow against our house. We had sold it a year earlier and were living in a two-bedroom rental at the time. I didn't even mention all the bills and other financial obligations at home. Those don't stop, you know. It was a tough, tough time. We were some broke-assed people!

After almost a year living like hermits, we were ready to move on to something—*anything*—that didn't involve a business model where all you do is pay bills. The restaurant was still very profitable, but enough was enough. We even went so far as to list the restaurant for sale with a broker. We'd made up our minds: We were getting out of the food business, this time for good.

In the meantime, the only thing we could do was claw our way out, day by day, week by week. There was no Monopoly money, there were no loans, no wealthy in-laws to save us. We just had to go back to how it was in the beginning: being in the store, watching every penny, saying please and thank you to our guests, and praying they'd come back through the door. Eventually, things got better. Our risky investment paid off, the credit cards got paid down, the vendors' invoices got caught up, our terms got reinstated, and the staff got their hours back. Calmer heads prevailed and we removed the listing with the broker. The following year's sales at the restaurant came in at one of our top three. The kids got new shoes for school and I got the van fixed. But it was hell—the hardest year we've been in this business. We've never forgotten that experience.

Chapter 15: Things Fall Apart (The Lifestyle, Part II)

> **NOTE**
> Even if you're established and have a forecastable income, you must not overextend yourself financially in your business or personal life. Expanding your business too soon or making major personal investments will come back to bite you in the ass if you're not careful. Things can change overnight—and your cash flow along with them.

Unfortunately, this scenario is not uncommon. It can happen to any restaurant operator. Even if you do all the right things, a sharp deviation in sales or a risky personal move can ruin everything you've worked for. The sad thing is, it may happen literally overnight, even for the most experienced. The math doesn't make allowances or distinguish between bad choices or even bad luck. It simply is what it is. This is why you'll see what seem to be busy restaurants that have been open for a number of years suddenly close.

How much it cost you to launch your restaurant will come back to visit you at some point. Whether you did it expensively or on the cheap will likely sink you or save you. We cannot stress enough the importance of taking plenty of time to plan. Inevitably, something will shift in your life, business, or both. If you've fortified yourself as much as possible, you may survive—and in some cases come out of it stronger and more focused than ever.

> **NOTE**
> During our journey, Erin and I have had it both ways. Sometimes, there has been zero debt and we could do what we wanted to do, when we wanted to do it. We have even sat on our living-room floor surrounded by piles of cash, like in one of those drug-smuggler movies. But there have been times when we've sold off personal items, maxed out credit, and refinanced or sold our real estate. At some point, it all goes with the territory.

Dealing with Down Times

More than likely, you *will* run up against financial trouble with your business. If you find yourself in a difficult period in which business is down but solvent, there is hope. If, however, business is down and you were barely squeaking by to begin with, you need to seriously consider how much you can stand before what could very well be a wrap. Ask yourself, even if you rebound, will it make a big enough difference? Or have you been taken hostage by the business and there's apparently no real way out of the abyss?

Regardless, when you're in the shit, the first step is to not lie to yourself. You must admit you are indeed in the shit. Sit down somewhere with a pencil, paper, and the most important piece of equipment you will ever buy for your restaurant, a calculator. Spread everything out on the table, with your favorite beverage within reach. You'll need to drill down as much as possible to where the money is going and where there are savings to be had. In other words, spend the day with your profit and loss (P&L) statement and study it like a habitual truant before finals week.

Your P&L Statement

Let's highlight some things to monitor. I've included two of our actual P&L statements—one good and one not so good. You or your bookkeeper should generate these every month. Fortunately, they're very simple to read.

First, the not-so-good statement:

Boogie Burger
Income and Expenses
January 31, 2012

	1 Month Ended January 31, 2012	1 Month Ended January 31, 2012	Percentages Month	YTD
SALES				
310 – Food	54,289.18	54,289.18	100.3	100.3
390 – T-shirts	67.78	67.78	0.1	0.1
396 – Refunds	(1.09)	(1.09)	0.0	0.0
398 – Coupons/Discounts	(240.94)	(240.94)	(0.4)	(0.4)
TOTAL SALES	54,114.93	54,114.93	100.0	100.0
COST OF SALES				
410 – Food Purchases	21,036.59	21,036.59	38.9	38.9
430 – Wages	19,894.95	19,894.95	36.8	36.8

Chapter 15: Things Fall Apart (The Lifestyle, Part II)

TOTAL COST OF SALES	40,931.54	40,931.54	75.6	75.6
GROSS PROFIT	13,183.39	13,183.39	24.4	24.4
OPERATING EXPENSES				
507 – Pest Control	25.00	25.00	0.0	0.0
512 – Freight/Postage	234.76	234.76	0.4	0.4
516 – Officers' Salaries	4,300.00	4,300.00	7.9	7.9
520 – Rent	2,634.42	2,634.42	4.9	4.9
526 – Utilities	975.76	975.76	1.8	1.8
530 – Repairs/Maintenance	379.28	379.28	0.7	0.7
534 – Advertising	225.00	225.00	0.4	0.4
535 – Insurance	628.30	628.30	1.2	1.2
542 – FICA Tax	1,996.69	1,996.69	3.7	3.7
543 – Unemployment Tax	304.05	304.05	0.6	0.6
551 – Bank Charges	107.51	107.51	0.2	0.2
552 – Vehicle Expense	97.27	97.27	0.2	0.2
558 – Contributions	65.00	65.00	0.1	0.1
564 – Legal/Professional	296.00	296.00	0.5	0.5
565 – ADP Invoices	274.30	274.30	0.5	0.5
566 – Office Expense	852.70	852.70	1.6	1.6
568 – Credit Card Discounts	1,227.67	1,227.67	2.3	2.3
574 – Amortization	301.75	301.75	0.6	0.6
575 – Depreciation	1,110.00	1,110.00	2.1	2.1
581 – Uniforms/Laundry	157.89	157.89	0.3	0.3
597 – Cash Over/Short	28.34	28.34	0.1	0.1
TOTAL OPERATING EXPENSE	16,221.69	16,221.69	30	30

PROFIT	(3,038.30)	(3,038.30)	(5.6)	(5.6)
OTHER INCOME				
901 – Interest Earned	0.08	0.08	0.0	0.0
920 – Gift Card Sales	10.00	10.00	0.0	0.0
930 – Grease Dump	329.30	329.30	0.6	0.6
TOTAL OTHER INCOME	339.38	339.38	0.6	0.6
OTHER EXPENSES				
960 – Gift Cards Redeemed	379.66	379.66	379.7	379.7
TOTAL OTHER EXPENSES	379.66	379.66	379.7	379.7
PROFIT	(3,078.58)	(3,078.58)	(5.7)	(5.7)

Now, the good statement:

Boogie Burger
Income and Expenses
March 31, 2012

	1 Month Ended March 31, 2012	3 Month Ended March 31, 2012	Percentages	
			Month	YTD
SALES				
310 – Food	94,902.50	232,288.37	100.3	100.3
390 – T-shirts	177.93	382.17	0.2	0.2
396 – Refunds	(34.71)	(92.02)	0.0	0.0
398 – Coupons/Discounts	(389.20)	(1,037.70)	(0.4)	(0.4)
TOTAL SALES	94,656.52	231,540.82	100.0	100.0
COST OF SALES				
410 – Food Purchases	27,732.92	84,188.50	29.3	36.4
420 – Paper Goods	435.15	1,486.07	0.5	0.6

Chapter 15: Things Fall Apart (The Lifestyle, Part II)

430 – Wages	20,331.87	59,968.58	21.5	25.9
TOTAL COST OF SALES	48,499.94	145,643.15	51.2	62.9
GROSS PROFIT	46,156.58	85,897.67	48.8	37.1
OPERATING EXPENSES				
507 – Pest Control	25.00	75.00	0.0	0.0
508 – Security	0.00	52.00	0.0	0.0
509 – Outside Services	0.00	50.00	0.0	0.0
510 – Operating Supplies	127.49	410.57	0.1	0.2
512 – Freight/Postage	0.00	234.76	0.0	0.1
516 – Officers' Salaries	3,600.00	11,500.00	3.8	5.0
520 – Rent	5,268.84	7,903.26	5.6	3.4
521 – Equipment Rental	0.00	301.34	0.0	0.1
526 – Utilities	1,055.74	3,687.37	1.1	1.6
529 – Telephone	175.26	348.37	0.2	0.2
530 – Repairs/Maintenance	836.00	1,826.07	0.9	0.8
534 – Advertising	50.00	1,617.14	0.1	0.7
535 – Insurance	691.00	1,073.00	0.7	0.5
536 – Health Insurance	437.30	1,311.90	0.5	0.6
538 – Meals/Entertainment	57.30	387.91	0.1	0.2
542 – FICA Tax	1,948.85	5,871.48	2.1	2.5
543 – Unemployment Tax	376.84	2,188.07	0.4	0.9
548 – Licenses/Permits	0.00	432.00	0.0	0.2
551 – Bank Charges	47.69	182.48	0.1	0.1
552 – Vehicle Expense	54.09	453.59	0.1	0.2
558 – Contributions	69.83	719.83	0.1	0.3

564 – Legal/Professional	0.00	719.50	0.0	0.3
564 – Bookkeeping	296.00	938.00	0.3	0.4
565 – ADP Invoices	109.04	495.00	0.1	0.2
566 – Office Expense	(16.30)	538.82	0.0	0.2
568 – Credit Card Discounts	1,715.90	4,222.66	1.8	1.8
574 – Amortization	301.75	905.25	0.3	0.4
575 – Depreciation	1,110.00	3,330.00	1.2	1.4
581 – Uniforms/Laundry	212.81	567.52	0.2	0.2
597 – Cash Over/Short	187.63	430.79	0.2	0.2
TOTAL OPERATING EXPENSE	19,124.66	53,933.48	20.2	23.3
PROFIT	27,031.92	31,964.19	28.6	13.8
OTHER INCOME				
901 – Interest Earned	0.47	0.87	0.0	0.9
920 – Gift Card Sales	111.89	166.89	0.1	0.1
930 – Grease Dump	302.60	1,074.20	0.3	0.5
TOTAL OTHER INCOME	414.96	1,241.96	0.4	0.5
OTHER EXPENSES				
960 – Gift Cards Redeemed	288.07	874.63	288.1	874.6
TOTAL OTHER EXPENSES	288.07	874.63	288.1	874.6
PROFIT	27,158.81	32,331.52	28.7	14.0

Let's start with the not-so-good statement, ending on January 31. Toward the top, you see our total sales. Below that are our cost of sales, total cost of sales, and gross profit. If you look in the top-right corner of the statement, you'll also see a "Percentages" heading followed by columns for the month and year to date (YTD). For this particular month, our percentages for food purchases and wages were 38.9% and 36.8%, for a total of almost 76%. This is horrible. The general rule of thumb is these two numbers should total no more than 65%. The operating expenses (which can vary month to month)

Chapter 15: Things Fall Apart (The Lifestyle, Part II)

follow. Whatever profit was left after food costs and labor is deducted by all the items you see going down the page. As you can see, our total operating expense for that month was $16,221.69, but our gross profit was $13,183.39. In other words, we lost about $3,000.

The statement ending March 31 presents a totally different story. Our total sales were higher and our food purchases and labor costs came in much lower, for a combined prime number of 51.2%—well below the 65% threshold. The gross profit was higher, so the operating expenses didn't kick us in the butt as bad as in January. After deducting those expenses, there was actually a pretty nice profit for that month.

At various times, your statements will resemble both of the examples here. Don't panic when it looks like January and don't celebrate when it looks like March. Monitor them and look for savings, leakage, and ways to keep your numbers in line. A quick look at these statements reveals we spent about the same on food purchases and wages in both months, but our ratios were out of whack. That tells me in January, we had too many people on the clock and bought way too much product—two easily fixable things.

> **TIP**
> Review your statements as soon as they come in and make adjustments sooner rather than later!

A Sample Scenario

Say you operate a mom and pop quick-service sandwich joint, similar to Sally's Soups and Sandwiches back in Chapter 4, "A Sample Business Plan." You're open every day from 11 a.m. to 11 p.m.

Just to keep the doors open on a daily basis costs a certain fixed amount. For the sake of example, let's say you're working with the following:

- **Rent:** $3,000 per month, or $100 per day
- **Front-of-house labor (two six-hour shifts, three cashiers per shift, each cashier paid $9 per hour):** $27 per hour × 12 hours = $324 per day
- **Back-of-house labor (two six-hour shifts, three cooks per shift, each cook paid $12 per hour):** $36 per hour × 12 hours = $432 per day
- **Total labor:** $756 per day
- **Electric:** $1,000 per month or $33 per day
- **Gas:** $800 per month or $27 per day

- **Insurance:** $150 per month or $5 per day
- **Internet/phone:** $200 per month or $7 per day

Already, you are over $900 a day, just to pay the basics. I'll stop here, but you get the idea. You can cost out other items such as linen service, pest control, trash service, etc. Credit card–processing fees will vary based on volume, but you still pay for them every day. Cash-sucking maintenance and equipment repairs will also crop up. If you were to break it down into as much minutia as you could, your average daily cost to operate this particular concept could be around $1,200. That's your number. Anything above that, and you're getting into profit. Anything less than that, and you're losing money. (And no, I did not include *your* salary.)

> **NOTE**
>
> If you're a corporate catering operation rather than a restaurant, your labor numbers may be lower because you'll likely have shorter workdays and no weekends. In addition, your lease and utilities may be cheaper. (See why catering is a little kinder to the operator?)

As the owner, it's your responsibility to stay on top of your numbers and to be present enough to know when it's time for an immediate pullback or adjustment. Go through everything with a fine-tooth comb and see where you can make the biggest cuts that will be the least disruptive to your operation.

If you've crunched numbers and decide it makes sense to close on a Monday or Sunday, then fine. Just be sure to post your new hours. If your cost of goods sold (COGS) percentage is out of whack, you may need to raise your prices. The public understands prices are always going up. If you've operated your business with sincerity and respect, these price hikes will be an easier sell. If, however, your place has gotten out of control due to your neglect, it will be much harder. You may even run off the already-shrinking guest base.

No matter what, you don't want to give the appearance that you've given up. You see the places that are going downhill. The trash cans stay full a little too long. The windows don't appear to have been washed in weeks. Maybe they answer the phone, maybe they don't. Nobody's picked up the cigarette butts around the front door or sidewalk for days. There's an overall feeling of sadness and despair. Don't let your place get to that point. Instead, keep your house in tip-top shape. At the very least, you must

Chapter 15: Things Fall Apart (The Lifestyle, Part II)

make sure your place is clean, the staff is friendly, and a certain air of pride remains (even if you are dead-assed broke).

What if you've trimmed everything you can, the place is immaculate, and you're *still* coming up short? Business is steady enough that you don't quite have to close, but until the weather breaks or you unstick yourself from whatever financial jam you're in, the heat is on. One false move could end everything. Well, in this case, there's a dance you'll have to do from month to month until the storm passes—a "frugality shuffle," if you will. It's difficult and it's humbling, but it happens all the time. Others have gotten through it and you can too.

> **NOTE**
>
> After you're around for a while, you'll notice concepts coming and going, local or national. You will notice huge sums of money spent, only to see them close in a short time. Or they may never seem to be busy yet stick around in expensive leases for years and even open more locations. Others are perpetually winning with all concepts in all locations. How is this done? There is no complicated answer. The math either works or it doesn't, for the taco stand or the 3,000-square-foot sports bar. Math does not discriminate.

Keeping Up with Payments

Just because you're in the shit doesn't mean there aren't still people who need to get paid. While these folks may be empathetic, in the end, they couldn't care less what you're going through. They want their money, and rightfully so.

So, what do you do if you don't have the money to pay everyone on your list? In my view, here's who you need to focus on, in this order:

- Your department(s) of revenue (a.k.a. "the tax man")
- Your vendors
- Your employees
- Your landlord

Of course, you may not be able to pay all these people on time. That's OK. You may incur penalties for being late, but as long as you pay eventually, you'll be fine.

Paying Your Taxes

Why do I prioritize paying the tax man? Simple. At the most extreme, you can go to jail for not paying your taxes. Not so if you don't pay your vendors, employees, or landlord. Less traumatic—but nevertheless embarrassing—is having a sheriff mosey into your business to perform a "till tap," literally taking money from your cash register. (This often happens on a weekend night, when you've likely got cash.) It's a bit like what you see in those old black-and-white gangster movies or westerns. It's perfectly legal, and there isn't a damn thing you can do about it. The tax man can also freeze your bank accounts.

Paying Vendors

At this point, cash is king. Naturally, you need to hold on to as much of it as you can for as long as you can until more comes in. Hopefully, you've negotiated the best terms possible with your vendors up front and have at least two weeks or more before payments on invoices are considered late. You may only have been granted a week. Whatever it is, you should have been offered some terms based on your credit application. (Remember the "Getting Your Finances in Order" chapter?)

> **TIP**
>
> Get the longest terms you can with each vendor at the very start, even if you never need that much time. That way, if the time ever comes when you *do* need it, the arrangements are already in place and in writing.

To be blunt, your only allegiance is to your profit-and-loss statement. If that means delaying payments to vendors, so be it. It will not be the first time they've dealt with it. Just don't be surprised if those pop-in visits by your sales rep become a bit less friendly!

Paying Your Staff

Obviously, you can't operate a restaurant by yourself. Your employees are your backbone. Still, payroll may be killing you. Sometimes, you may simply not be able to pay it on time. If you can help it, try to avoid this.

Then again, if you do have to miss payroll, don't beat yourself up too bad. Again, it won't be the first or the last time it's happened in the foodservice industry. Don't let it happen too often, though, and don't be too late. Paying your staff a day or so late is acceptable by most standards, but any longer than that, and there'll be trouble on the

Chapter 15: Things Fall Apart (The Lifestyle, Part II)

horizon. Your loyal soldiers may stick by your side for a brief period, but these people have bills and obligations, too. Like anyone else, their self-preservation will take priority over your business. Besides, by virtue of the fact they work in the foodservice industry, these are people already missing out on perks like sick days and paid vacations.

The danger with being late with payroll—particularly if it becomes a habit—is the breakdown of morale and trust that ensues. If you're late with their money, you may never get a decent shift's work from them again. After all, they think, why should they continue to work hard when you obviously don't care about their security? The best people will leave the quickest—and those who remain only stick around because they're stealing.

It may be that you can manage to make payroll—but only if you lay people off. If you have to start laying people off because you can't afford to pay them any longer, do what you have to do—but do it sooner rather than later. It'll be best for both of you.

Paying Your Landlord

Landlords of commercial real estate—specifically restaurant properties—are used to getting paid late. Often, they're paid months late…if at all. More often than not, when a tenant goes out of business, the landlord is owed thousands of dollars. This is nothing new to landlords. It's the risk they assume when they own this type of property.

The lucky ones with the best locations land national tenants who sign 20 plus–year leases backed by the corporate office. The majority, however, are mom and pops who own a building here or there or perhaps a modest strip mall in the city limits. Every now and then they'll hit pay dirt with a long-term tenant, but the best most of them can hope for is a hefty up-front deposit from new tenants, have the tenants improve their building, and have their real estate taxes paid. Sometimes, they'll also wind up in possession of furniture or equipment left behind after a tenant closes that they can sell. They know in time there will always be another yahoo who wants to open a restaurant, at which point they'll start the process all over again.

All this is to say that if you get behind with your landlord, believe me, he or she will understand. Most landlords will work with you in situations like these. After all, they'd much rather see you stick around—at least until they can get someone else lined up. They dislike vacancies as much as you dislike an empty dining room. Have an honest chat about your situation. Work out a deal to pay something until you get things back together if he or she is willing. Eventually, you'll need to be prepared for your landlord to evict and/or sue you for non-payment.

Closing Your Doors

At some point, every restaurant will reach its maturation point. When it does, revenues will be fairly predictable or may even go down. Even if you've done all the right things over the years, there may come a time when you have to work with less. Increased competition from new restaurants, a shift in tastes, or simply guest fatigue can all contribute to lower sales. If you find yourself in this position, whatever you do, don't start discounting your menu or giving things away. You'll look desperate. Your brand deserves to stand strong and command a fair price for the value you give.

> **TIP**
>
> As your brand settles into maturity, look at the sales from your best year. Then ask yourself whether you can continue working with 80%, 70%, or less of that number.

Of course, this begs the question that no one wants to ask: When is it time to close? This is a matter of your threshold for personal and financial pain. However, I'll be the first to say you should do it sooner rather than later. Smart businesspeople know when to cut their losses.

> **NOTE**
>
> For what it's worth, I've observed women are much more practical than men in this area. When the writing's on the wall, they close shop and move on. Often, men's egos and pride make them cling to a loser for far too long. They will put up a front for months—sometimes years—to save face, all the while pumping money into a dying dog. After a long, slow decline, they finally put the thing out of its misery. Inevitably, they blame the closure on everything other than their stubbornness.

If you've been present and accounted for an entire year or year and half, taken the greatest care to open your place in as financially prudent a manner as possible, watched labor and food costs like a hawk, and aren't profitable, then get out. I say a year or more because that way, you've given yourself a chance to get through all four seasons. Unless you or an investor have more cash to pump in, stop the bleeding and move on.

Chapter 15: Things Fall Apart (The Lifestyle, Part II)

On the other hand, if, after the same length of time, you're breaking even or are a little on the plus side, then there's something there. If your city's population is big enough, there's still hope. With a little more time and exposure, you may hit your stride and earn your place in the landscape (and the sales that come with it).

We've seen dozens of places come and go, right in our neighborhood. It's always a downer to see them close. But whenever I bump into an ex-owner, which happens every now and then, most of them have a look of peace on their face. It's like the joke about the two happiest days in a boat owner's life: the day they buy it and the day they sell it.

A few years ago, the restaurant next door to our original location got into some trouble. Ultimately, this 20-year landmark in one of the most popular neighborhoods in the city closed down after a long and painful descent. (Our opinion is it held on too long to the $100 a person, two-hour meal during the depths of the recession, but this is us looking in from the outside.) Some Monday and Tuesday nights, they would have one table. *One.* Thursday, Friday, and Saturday were better, but not good enough—especially since we heard their rent was close to $8,000 a month. There was a small nightclub on the second floor open weekends, but I don't think it really made a dent. As they got deeper and deeper in the shit, various vendors and utility providers, looking to collect on invoices or disconnect services, would stumble into our place, asking for the whereabouts of the owner or manager. I'd explain that they didn't open until 5 p.m., so they'd have to try back later. Surprisingly, every time I saw the owner, he was calm and collected—even at the very end. I will say, he didn't go out without a fight.

If you're in this situation, don't close your doors without trying to sell the business first. That way, you'll at least get *something*, even if it's just for the liquor license. If there aren't any takers—sometimes there just isn't a buyer—then thank your guests, shut the doors, and get some sleep, which you probably deserve. Most importantly, don't feel bad. You were a part of one of the oldest and toughest businesses out there. If you were able to make a go of it even for a little while, you did better than the 90% who talk about doing it but never actually do. (For more on selling your business, see Chapter 16, "Moving, Expanding, and Selling.")

Interview with Chef Allen Shideler

How long have you been a professional in the restaurant industry?

25 years.

What attracted you? Why did you want to become a chef?

I just knew I'd be a chef. Never had to think about it. Just knew when I was in high school that that what I was going to do. My dad dabbled in selling to restaurants. He made homemade salsa, homemade sausage, and I just knew that's what I'd do. I grew up on a farm and I like the mix of business and farm and I just knew I'd be a chef. Sometimes you just know what you're going to do, like you know where you parked your car at the mall. You know what I mean? When you walk out, you know where it is because that's where you parked it. You just know.

What do you like least about the business?

People suck. Customers want this, that. They want to play "create your own menu." Employees, they don't show up. They don't have the same passion as you do.

Have you found in recent years a lot of people get into the culinary profession because of the popularity of TV shows, etc.?

Exactly. They think it's glamorous.

And it's not that glamorous, is it?

Oh yeah, if you got your own TV show.

What's the biggest mistake you've seen owners make over the years that was directly or indirectly responsible for them struggling?

Real estate. You have a building and you rent it. A lot of times, in the restaurant business, the restaurant owner is responsible for upkeep and taxes. He's responsible for everything and just gives the landlord a check. They don't inspect the building. They don't have a professional inspection or even inspect it themselves. They don't go in the crawlspace or basement. They don't realize, well, the floor is rotted or there's termites or water damage. They sign on the dotted line. Don't own a restaurant unless you own the building! I know it's hard, but don't own a restaurant unless you own the building.

Chapter 15: Things Fall Apart (The Lifestyle, Part II)

I remember you always said that.

Don't get me wrong, I know there's money to be made renting. I mean, if you have a long-term lease, like 10 years, that's great. But when you have somebody that says, "This went up, that went up...."

On the flip side, tell me about a place you've worked where things went right. What did those owners do?

There's no such thing.

Well, tell me about a place that stayed solvent and had continuity. What's kept them around? The food costs, the fixed costs? Marketing?

Morale. As far as morale goes, if you hire somebody to do a job let, them do it. So many people—especially owners—hire somebody to do a job, and they want to micromanage them. They're a wanna-be chef or a wanna-be bar manager. They hire somebody, but they come in and say, "Oh, well, do this, do that." They're not qualified to do it themselves because they had to hire a chef or hire somebody, you know what I mean? At first, that would aggravate me. But then I got to the point where I just let them do it. You're going to pay me, but then you're going to do part of my job? Have at it! I've opened four restaurants and every time I open a restaurant, when it's in the process of opening, they let me do my thing. But once it's open, all the work's done and it's up and running, *then* they want to come back and say, "Oh, well, put some more potatoes on that plate or put some more vegetables on that plate." When the kitchen was being built and there were no outlets in the walls, and I said to the construction company, "Well, I have blenders, food processors," the owner didn't have anything to say. But when everything is done and it's all laid out, *then* they want to come back and act like they know something. Now they know about the restaurant business. "Shouldn't the fish portion be 7 ounces instead of 8 or 6 ounces?" I've had extremes. I've had, like, really bad, and I've had "blessed be me."

We were neighbors way back when and I know the place where you worked had some difficulties at the end. I left work one day and saw a huge gas grill in the parking lot at the back door.

From what I remember, the owner gave us some poppycock about a problem with the gas. It wasn't, "I didn't pay the bill," but we knew he didn't pay the bill, so the gas was shut off. We just went and rented a grill, like you would to cater. We just grilled the steaks outside and took them inside to plate them. We still had electricity, so we could use the microwave for some of the sides. We just didn't have any gas. We were sautéing out there, too. There were a few little pastas, some fish.

The guests were none the wiser huh?

No, they didn't know.

So you guys punk-rocked it.

You know, you do what you gotta do to pay the bills. Or not pay the bills. Whichever you choose.

Say you're approached by some owners who want to open a restaurant. What would you tell them to consider if they want to stick around?

Own the building. Start small. Do 50 to 60 seats so you can be busy all the time. Sure, the weekends you'll be on a wait, but that's OK. You really don't need more than 80 seats. Or, go 30 or 40 seats and be packed, and people will be like, "Man, we can't ever get in there." But if you have the money to open a restaurant, put it in the bank and don't open a restaurant.

You're opening your own restaurant. What does it look like?

High-end, average 25 to 30 seats. Small bar, beer and wine license only, because they're inexpensive and with the whole craft-beer and local-wine thing now, that's all you need. No need to serve liquor. Price point...most expensive entrée low to mid 20s. You know, be busy all the time. Lunch and dinner if you're in a good location. Steaks, fish, variations on potato dishes.

Chapter 16

Moving, Expanding, and Selling

By now, you've been around three or more years. Not surprisingly, you've seen a number of restaurants come and go. The flurry of restaurant openings and closings makes your head spin. Some closed within a year, others after their third winter, and most somewhere in between. You've seen various national big brands come to town, spend millions on a buildout, only to close it down two years later. Inevitably, they walk away from a brand-new building and open the same damn thing on the other side of town. "Why?" you wonder. And, "How?"

When you look around your shop, you figure whatever you're doing must be working. It's kept you around this long (even if it did damn near kill you to get to this point). Trust me, if you've been in business three years or longer, congratulations are in order! You know by now how slim the margins are, you've survived a few rough winters, and you've quickly educated yourself about debt service. You've faced down new competition and learned to manage people. Maybe you've outgrown your space and want to move into bigger digs. Maybe you're ready to open another storefront. Or perhaps it's time to sell and move on to the next concept. It's your hard work to leverage, any way you'd like!

Moving the Business

If business is good, you're having a ball, and you need larger space, you're in a great position! Most places live and die where they start. Moving takes guts, not to mention having confidence the risk and expense of moving will pay off. We've moved two different businesses. Both times, the move made sense in our opinion. One was much easier than the other, but both came out winners, and that's all that matters.

The first was the catering business. Moving it was a breeze. It was just a matter of timing it around weekends and a few weekdays to move everything over. (Again, the beauty of catering is you can be on the damn *moon* and nobody cares—as long as you're on time with the food!)

The second was the burger joint. This was a bit trickier. We'd definitely outgrown our location. Our space was quaint, but no longer practical. For one thing, it had no storage. We had room for maybe two days' worth of inventory—and even that was a stretch. That meant constantly running around to replenish stock. There were other challenges, too. Despite its small space, gas and electric bills for the location ran high. Plus, the neighborhood was always congested with all the delivery trucks and vans, not to mention residents and visitors. Getting to our place was becoming harder and harder, and parking was nearly impossible. Still, the numbers made it worth dealing with it all.

Initially, we felt it made sense to open a second location. After all, we'd long received visitors from surrounding suburbs who told us they loved the place and wished we'd open one nearer to them. The market wasn't too crowded yet, so we figured, yeah, why not? If we could make this thing work in what amounted to a closet, with no parking, no air conditioning, and just 13 seats, we could make it could work anywhere. Erin and I spent about a year canvassing different spaces around town, updating our business plan, and envisioning how everything would work staffing- and management-wise. We probably looked at 10 spaces.

It was fun at first, but after a while, the more we saw, the less interested we became. We had no doubt another location would rock. And of course, the extra money would be great. But when we thought about another lease on top of our existing one plus the associated utilities and other fixed costs with a seven-days-a-week operation—not to mention the inevitable headaches with employees—the juice didn't seem worth the squeeze. Plus, we'd have to give up another two or three years of our lives to make it work, which wasn't an attractive prospect. Our kids were still very young, and I'd already missed out on a lot of dinners, parties, and get-togethers covering for no-show workers or running around to pick up inventory. In my mind, no amount of money was worth missing being together as a family. So it was decided. If there were to be more burger joints, we'd be a franchisor. But we weren't going to open any new stores ourselves. We stopped looking for a second location and agreed moving the existing business to a larger space would be a better fit.

We had to come to grips with the fact that we'd very likely have to leave our neighborhood, which despite the challenges, we loved so much. For one thing, it was unlikely we'd be able to find a space there that a) already had a kitchen built in, b)

Chapter 16: Moving, Expanding, and Selling

offered decent terms, and c) had adequate storage—our three main requirements. But we kept an eye out for restaurants in the area that were open but struggling.

Around November or December, our new place revealed itself to us. The funny thing was, we'd been driving past it nearly every day for the past four years. The building had been constructed as a restaurant sometime in the 1960s. It was owned and operated by a family with a wholesome Midwestern theme of tenderloin sandwiches, soups, salads, and general American casual fare—with a twist (for real). Called the Tin Star Jail, its shtick was a jailhouse theme complete with booths in the basement encased in jail cells. When you arrived, you were "locked" into your "cell" and given menus. After ordering, a server delivered a hearty jailhouse meal to you. When you were finished, your guest check arrived in the form of "bail." After you paid (and presumably tipped), you were free to go. (At least, that's how the concept was explained to me by neighborhood folks. Sadly, I never ate there before the end of their run, which lasted a good 30 or 40 years.)

After the Tin Star Jail closed, the building hosted a series of concepts from BBQ to pizza, all having short lifespans. The most recent incarnation had a late-night diner theme. Clearly, it had been on the ropes for a while. In its waning days, Erin and I reviewed the positives: The building was old but functional. It had its own parking lot with about 25 spaces. The kitchen was already in place. Because the building was built to be a restaurant, all the plumbing and electrical infrastructure was A+. There was also a walk-in cooler and a full basement ideal for storage. (The jail cells had since been removed.) All this, and it was only a mile or so east of our current location. In fact, it was located on the street that fed into that neighborhood's main drag.

We found the address of the property owner and sent a letter introducing ourselves and letting him know we'd be interested in the space should it become available. No reply. After a few weeks, just as we predicted, the current tenant closed shop. Still no answer from the owner. Admittedly, I got a little antsy. I assumed another operator was thinking what we were thinking and had already tied up the property. But Erin was like, "Please. Nobody wants to touch that place. There've been four different restaurants there in six years." "Yeah, yeah," I said. "But why lose out?" So we called our broker friend Catherine and got her on the case.

Catherine had no problem setting up a showing with the owner a few days later. When we arrived, we quickly saw that for us, the place was perfect—or as perfect as we were going to find. Around 2,000 square feet, it fell right in line with what we thought the concept needed to function at its highest potential. There were separate restrooms and heavy-duty electric and HVAC systems. Hell, the previous tenant had even left behind furniture and equipment, which the landlord was happy to sell. It didn't make sense not to take it.

After we got a lease together, it was time to announce we were moving. Were we ever unprepared for the backlash! The doom and gloom expressed to us personally and on social media was definitely a downer. Some people rooted for our failure. "The place is cursed. Nothing survives in there." "You'll lose all your foot traffic and neighborhood customers." "Well it looks like that's the end for them." Many days, Erin came home upset and worried. She worked the front, so she got the brunt of the naysayers' doomsday predictions. I can't say it didn't give me pause, too, but the length of that pause was the same length of time it took you to read this sentence.

Anybody with half a brain knew it made perfect sense to move. And there were plenty of people who *did* understand what we were doing and gave us encouragement. True, after the run of the initial owners, the new place had had a string of failures. But I so badly wanted to reply to the doubters, "What the fuck does that have to do with us? The foot traffic we'd 'lose' down the street came to this neighborhood by car—right past our new location!" (Instead, I just said, "I hope you'll join us when it opens and we look forward to serving you in a more comfortable setting." That was the script.) Besides, anyone unwilling to make the trip down the street would be replaced by any number of the several thousand people who drove past on a daily basis.

Nope. We were moving, and that was that.

We moved in April and opened in early May. (Remember what I said about opening in the spring?) Were so damn busy, we ran out of food three times in the first week. (The first time it was kind of cute. After that, it got embarrassing. It showed me how being ill-prepared can catch you unawares, even if you've been through the motions before.) The moral of the story: If there is a kitchen, and you use it to produce something people want, and you manage your business as best as possible, then you can operate nearly anywhere.

> **TIP**
>
> People will offer all kinds of "expert" advice, despite knowing nothing about the inner workings of your operation. When they do, be polite and listen to their concerns and feedback—even if you don't agree. Although some just like to gossip and predict train wrecks, others do mean well. Regardless of what they say, go with your heart and stick to your goals.

Chapter 16: Moving, Expanding, and Selling

After you get settled in at your new location, don't be surprised if you hear folks lament how "Things have changed," or "The food isn't the same," or "You guys started cutting corners." Unless you are a complete and utter idiot, *nothing* will have changed (except your location, of course). Why would you change something that was working? We moved with the same staff, equipment, and menu, and even upgraded a few things. But, for whatever reason, some people thought the food tasted better in the old spot. All we could do was reassure them we were the same place, just inside different walls, and hope they'd give the new place a chance.

What's really important with a move is to adjust to your new overhead. Now, it may take six, seven, or eight people to run a shift instead of four or five, so your labor expense will increase. This is true even if you're dealing with a hot, slow July evening or a bitterly cold, short winter day. You may be tempted to cut staff, but rest assured you'll get busy out of nowhere and find yourself short. When you have a bigger space in a more visible location, you must be ready for 50 or 60 people at once, at any time. A bigger location will also have more trash to empty, higher utility bills, higher insurance, and higher common area maintenance (CAM) charges. Don't get sticker-shock.

Opening More Locations

Although Erin and I chose not to personally open a second location, opting instead to move, you may do the opposite. As you might guess, opening the second space involves the same steps as opening the first.

The good news is, opening a second storefront for your business will likely be easier and less expensive than opening the first one was. (This goes for moving, too.) Why? Because you know what need, what works, and what doesn't. When we started our catering business, we spent close to $100K to get up and running. When we moved that business to the building we bought, it set us back $50K, which included the down payment on the real estate. Like I said, less expensive. The same went for the burger joint. We paid about $80K in total to open ($60K of which went to the sellers). But when we moved to the new location, we were out of pocket no more than $50K.

> **TIP**
> Don't be afraid to take a chance if the numbers look good. If it's time to expand, expand. Or, if it's time to move, move.

You're not limited to running new stores yourself. You could franchise the concept or open turnkeys with management agreements. Then again, maybe you're ready to launch a variation of your original —for example, a food truck or catering arm. Or maybe you're ready to launch a new concept altogether. Whatever you decide, now that you've enjoyed some success, you may find investors are interested in your ideas. And if you're lucky, the bank may even talk to you!

A word of warning: If your primary location has gotten a lukewarm reception, think twice before you open a second one. We've seen restaurants open additional locations when there was clearly no demand. And just because you have the means to open more doesn't mean you should. I get the scaling strategy to capture share. But if it's done too quickly, all you wind up with is bills in two different places and unnecessary suffering because there was never a strong following to begin with. This occurs frequently.

Selling Your Business

If you're ready to sell your operation and you happen to own your building, you have a two options. One is to sell the real estate along with the business to boost your take and free yourself from landlord-related headaches. The other is to keep the real estate and enjoy the rental income it brings. The downside of option 2, of course, is the high failure rate with a niche product like restaurant property. Dealing with hassles over back rent, maintenance issues, and lawsuits may not appeal to a lot of people. And remember, if an operator gets into trouble, the landlord will always be the last to get paid (if he or she gets anything at all). Taking all that into consideration, I would *still* keep the real estate. After all, commercial leases can be structured with terms as advantageous to the landlord as you wish, with the tenant being responsible for nearly everything. If the right tenant makes a home in the space, it can work out beautifully for both parties.

Either way, you'll need to set an asking price for the business. What are your toil, blood, sweat, and tears over the last several years' worth? How do you value your good name and reputation? The quick down and dirty would be a multiple of net income or cash flow. In most cases, it's about three times, although you can set any price you wish with the ultimate worth decided on what a buyer is willing to pay. If you net $50K, it's not unreasonable to ask for $150K or a little more. Or, $100K in net income would generally command an asking price of $300K, etc.

Suppose your restaurant nets $100K to the bottom line. I'm an active buyer, and you're asking $300K (for the business only). I'm wagering that if nothing else changes, I should make my investment back in three years. In this business, three years can be an eternity. So it's risky. But if I've done my due diligence, considering every possible angle and circumstance, a deal could get done. Most sellers don't get asking price, however.

Chapter 16: Moving, Expanding, and Selling

Therefore, I would probably make an offer around $200K unless there was some real estate involved in the deal. In the end, we'd probably get a deal done somewhere between $200K and $250K, depending on how strong the brand is.

Looking back at our numbers, and after talking with other owners, the sweet spot to sell seems to be around years five and six. (Our best year with the burger joint was in year five. An industry friend told us to expect a dip around year seven, then a leveling to a new normal.) Getting out at year three is perfectly fine, but you could be leaving money on the table. Don't be surprised if your asking price gets beat down. It's really a matter of timing and if the stars and moon align in everyone's favor.

> **TIP**
>
> Of course, you should consult with your attorney and your accountant throughout the entire sales process!

Should you use a broker to market your business and find you a buyer? It's up to you. These days, with the power of technology, you can pretty much sell anything yourself. That being said, we hired a broker when we sold the catering company. He brought us a legit buyer in about 60 days, but we paid him 10%. (Ouch!) We also hired a broker when we listed the burger joint, although we came to our senses before selling it. Still, I don't think we would have done it any differently. For one thing, yes, brokers can be expensive, but their fees are negotiable. For another, experienced brokers in the restaurant world are plugged in many places and can probably connect you with a serious buyer a lot faster. Still, if your place is popular enough, maybe you don't need one. You can run your own campaign. All you'll have to deal with is accounting and legal fees.

If you're ready to get out, then sell. If you break even, you're left with no debt, and you were able to make a living for a few years, I'd call it a win. If you get out upside-down, then the business wasn't successful financially, but the wealth of knowledge you gained will be invaluable should you decide to give it another go. If you repeatedly lose money in the restaurant business, I strongly suggest another career.

Chapter 17

Dealing with Life Events

One day—it was in the fall—I was in the office doing paperwork. It was a regular morning. The burger joint had been in its new location for about seven months and things were humming right along. It looked like we were closing in on just shy of a million dollars in sales, which wasn't bad for a couple of people running out of unemployment five years earlier.

The phone rang. When I picked it up, I heard my wife on the other end of the line. She was sobbing. With some difficulty, she explained during a routine visit to her OB-GYN, they'd found a lump in her breast. They were going to do a biopsy to find out if it was cancer. It would be a week before they could get her in for the biopsy, and another week after that before we'd have the results. All we could do was wait. That was the worst—the waiting. It was like my brain couldn't stop spinning. Is it cancer? If so, how far along is it? How aggressive is it? And of course, why, why, why? I couldn't sleep. I couldn't eat. It was horrible. Sure enough, the lump was cancerous. We were blindsided. Nothing had showed up on her prior year's mammogram, and there was no family history of breast cancer.

In December, Erin had the first of what would total four surgeries. After the first surgery, while Erin recovered, her mom came to town and stayed with us to help with the kids. (One was still in pre-school and the other in second grade.) Erin would go back to the hospital two additional times over the next couple of months.

February rolled around. We'd made plans to attend a fundraiser for our son's school one Saturday evening—our first outing since Erin's surgeries. Thankful for our new beginning, we were excited to get out of the house and were looking forward to a good time.

Restaurant Winners

The plan was for my mother to come watch the kids while we were out. The morning of the event, I called her to firm up our plans but didn't get an answer. No big deal, I thought. She usually did her grocery shopping and ran errands on Saturday mornings. I figured I'd just stop by in a few hours, after I got done with my own running around.

Later that afternoon, I got to her apartment. Her car was in her parking space, so I knew she was home. I walked up to her door and knocked. No answer. I knocked again. Still no answer. After knocking for several minutes and no one answering, I got worried. I had a key to her apartment, but it was at home, about 10 minutes away. Nervously, I got back in my car and sped home to get it, all the while having a bad feeling.

When I got back to her apartment, I ran to her front door. My hands were shaking so bad, I had a hard time unlocking it. Finally, I got the door open…and my fears were confirmed. She was unconscious on the couch, slumped over, with dried blood caked around her nose.

I ran over to her and tried to pull her up, but she fell over in a heap. I called 911. "What do I do?!" I screamed at the operator. She told me to lift her off the couch and place her on the floor. Then she talked me through how to perform CPR, which I did while waiting for the ambulance.

Finally, the EMT's arrived. They confirmed she was still alive, but just barely. They asked me if I had a hospital preference and told me they'd take care of her as best they could. As they left with her, one of them hung back and told me, as delicately as he could, that I shouldn't drive recklessly on the way to the hospital. In other words, there was no need to rush.

After they were gone, I stood alone in her apartment, looking around. I saw the newspaper next to her, telling me she'd been in that condition since the previous morning. My guess was she'd been having her coffee and reading the paper. Why hadn't I checked on her yesterday? Why hadn't I stopped by? I beat myself up pretty bad. I felt so helpless.

I cried over how cruel the last chapter in her life was. My mother's' final years hadn't been the kindest. She'd suffered from serious episodes of depression and, I imagine, loneliness. I tried to be the best son I could be, I tried to help her through it, but we struggled year after year. Although her grandchildren brought a little light to her eyes, through the years, I often wondered if my mother was just…ready to go.

Chapter 17: Dealing with Life Events

Later, I learned she had suffered a massive aneurysm followed by a series of strokes. After emergency surgery and a week in the ICU, it was clear she had no chance of improving. The decision was made to remove life support and to let things take their course. She hung on for two more days in the hospital before being moved to hospice next door. There, she clung to life for another week before insurance required her to be moved again. This time it was to a long-term facility, where she died next day. This whole process was agonizing.

Of course, when you "let things take their course," it means you remove the patient's feeding tube. Watching my mother—who had always been a skinny little thing—basically turn into a skeleton before my eyes was unbearable. I had extreme feelings of guilt. I felt like I had starved her to death. Fortunately, there were professional people I could talk to, and they explained to me that this happens. They told me the transition to death—while not pleasant to watch—is just that: a transition. They assured me that Mom had been in no pain. I took care of all the funeral arrangements, contacting family members and what friends of hers I could locate.

A few weeks after Mom's burial, Erin had the last of her surgeries. I had literally spent the last five months in hospitals. Emotionally, there was nothing left in the tank. It felt like someone was constantly punching me, right below the sternum, from the time I woke up until the time I went to sleep. For some reason, I couldn't feel my legs. I just floated. Erin, our families, our children, and our friends were all that kept me going. One of my best friends, Kevin, who I'd known since we were six years old and who was the first friend I ever made in my neighborhood, called me nearly every day throughout this time, even though he was dealing with his own health issues. (He would also die two years later.)

Why do I tell you all this? Simple. I know that somebody, somewhere is going through something similar or worse. When these things happen, you may not feel like you can get out of bed, let alone run a business open seven days week with 15 employees. But the world keeps spinning and there are responsibilities to handle. As tempting as it may be to duck and cover, most times, it's not an option. We still had guests coming to the restaurant, surely dealing with their own problems. At the very least, we owed them open doors if we were able.

When Erin got sick, we met with the staff. We told them that during Erin's surgeries and recovery times, we'd be spending some time away from the shop. We asked our team to step up and look out for the place, and our good people did just that. (Unfortunately, our bad people did not. They took advantage of our situation by being lazy and even stealing. We dealt with that as best we could until we were able to fire them.) Throughout all Erin's surgeries and my mother's' death, the store never closed a day.

> **NOTE**
> Erin's hospital bills were well into the six figures. Fortunately, the year before, the restaurant had finally started doing well enough we were able to afford medical insurance. I guess you could say the foodservice industry saved our lives...for the second time.

To deal with these types of life events, make it a point to have your processes in place and in writing. Create any charts, manuals, or checklists you need and keep them updated. Ask yourself, can your operation fly on its own with minimal or even no participation on your part for a set amount of time? If so, how long could it go? A week? Three weeks? Months?

If things necessitate your absence and there isn't enough staff to run it without you, consider adjusting operating days and hours to fit around your new schedule. You'll have to find a way make things fit. No matter what, keep going as best you can. Things will eventually get better. Entrepreneurs are tough.

> **NOTE**
> Temporary closure when dealing with life events should be your last resort. But if you have no other choice, so be it.

How did we deal with what we were going through? We just...did. We kept our routine as normal as possible. We got up, ate breakfast, and took the kids to school. At work, I still ordered the inventory, and Erin still made the schedules. Moments alone in the car, the walk-in cooler, or at home were opportunities to scream, cry, think, or argue with God. In the end, the healing was in the work. I couldn't take time off to lay around the house and get it all "out"; I would never have left the house. We kept things going and went to work every day. That was all we could do.

Chapter 18

If You Sell to Foodservice People...

Not long ago, Erin and I—along with 40 or 50 other people—won a trip to Montego Bay, Jamaica from one of our broadline suppliers and their partners. To say that airfare plus five days and four nights at a five-star, all-inclusive resort in Jamaica during the middle of January was a generous gift for our loyalty is an understatement. Needless to say, we really like our rep and her company, which is employee-owned and "local."

During the trip, we met people in the various nooks and crannies of foodservice: a supplier to school systems, the purchasing manager for one of the largest hospitals in the city, brokers, and of course restaurateurs big and small, old and new. It was awesome meeting people like ourselves, all in one place. During our chats, we found every operator has his or her own equipment likes and dislikes, kitchen setups, and different ways to prep and cook. Everyone has different business hours and their own management styles. It was really cool to hear what works and what doesn't for others. We were proud to sit with these people—these job creators and community builders. We understood the price they were paying as well.

We shared stories about kooky guests and struggles with staff—how you bend over backward doing favors for employees during their personal emergencies or hardships, only to have them take advantage of the situation or talk shit about the restaurant or owners on the Internet when they're only (respectfully but rightly) asked to be accountable for their duties. We listened to a couple who, with their last restaurant move, purchased an historic building and built it out from a shell. The health department, variance committees, and city utilities drama gave them fits! We laughed at the absurdity of the restaurant TV shows that glossed over the real grit and pain involved. We talked about how you can go "all in" on your dream, which thrills the hell out of you and makes you sick to your stomach at the same time. We asked them if they had an exit strategy. Were they in it for the long haul or what? Their answer was what any entrepreneur would tell you: For the right price, "everything's" for sale.

It was certainly a nice gesture on the part of the company and manufacturers who sponsored the trip (who, as everyone knows, pull in billions of dollars a year from foodservice people across the land). But if you sell to people like us, you don't have to go quite that far to reward our loyalty. Trips are nice, but you can win business with the basics. This chapter offers a few other suggestions for getting and keeping our business.

Make an Appointment

OK, I'll admit: Operators can be high-strung. Often, it's hard to pin them down. And they're juggling a thousand different things at once. So yes, if you're selling to them, you need to find some way to stand out and get their attention. Often, however, salespeople interpret this to mean barging in on them unannounced.

I've had salespeople come in through unlocked back doors and stroll through the kitchen to chat up whoever they run into until they can grab a few minutes with me. It's like they appear out of nowhere. You turn a corner and *bam*! There they are, standing by the walk-in or three-bay sink, ready to talk product. I've also had salespeople come in at the worst possible times—around lunchtime, at the end of the week, when we were the busiest. One of our early broadline reps was notorious for this. I'm not sure if it was coincidence or a clever strategy, but almost every time it happened, I'd over-order, fail to confirm a price, or forget something crucial because I was in a hurry and I wanted to get him out of my face.

Nowadays, we insist on appointments. For a set amount of time—say, 30 minutes. That way, we can talk uninterrupted. Sometimes, reps try to get around this by bringing a manager or broker along with them for a cold call, saying they were "in the neighborhood." But I don't play. I don't need to drop everything I'm doing just because there're two of them. Not to mention, now they want me to listen to some clackety manager ask a bunch of questions or a broker who wants to sample yet another bag of sweet potato fries or chicken poppers? Nope.

Tell Us About Changes Ahead of Time

Another pet peeve is when a company discontinues or substitutes a product without warning. This is frustrating if you've grown to like something and it works well with your concept. But these things happen, and it's the operator's job to sell the menu. Still, it would be nice if salespeople gave a heads up as early as possible when a major product change is about to go down—even though they know I may have to switch to a competitor at least temporarily. I don't want a substitution on the truck without warning and us having a chance to test it.

> **NOTE**
> This goes back to Chapter 7, "A Sample Timeline to Opening Day," where I talked about getting set up with your vendors. When you're putting your menu together, the broader your category options, the greater your flexibility when vendors alter or discontinue items. Yes, I know. The more scratch cooking, the better. But you won't be arrested for serving frozen cheese sticks.

Help Us Find Ways to Save

Once, I was invited to speak to a group of salespeople. I asked them what *their* pet peeves about operators were. To a person, the answer was whining about high prices and no loyalty. They explained that while there was pricing flexibility, it was not as simple as owners would like to believe. "Well," I told them, "there are some things you *can* do and some things you *can't*." What I meant was, their customer may be in a situation where food costs aren't the real problem.

If you sell to restaurants, try to uncover the *real* reason for each operator's angst over the bottom line. Assuming the operator is willing to share information, a few minutes of detective work on your part may reveal your company's "high prices" are just a bit player in the grand scheme of things. See if the operator will let you look at his or her P&L statement. This may help you uncover other problem areas besides the food bill. For example, if the operator's rent expense is 10% and labor is 40%, that person is already under pressure. Rent should be less than 5% and labor around 30%. If those expenses are out of whack, that poor operator doesn't stand a chance.

> **NOTE**
> If you can help to shift the blame for massive monthly expenses to the gamut of other players involved *besides* you, that person will view you as ally rather than adversary. Uncover as much as you can, offer whatever restaurant rescue services your company has available, and tell the operator there is hope (if there is), and you'll be seen as a partner—part of an "us versus them" team (the "them" being everybody else).

Remember: An operator pays loads of bills every month. Among these, however, there is only *one* rent bill, *one* gas bill, *one* electric bill, *two* payrolls, and so on. In contrast, that operator may receive anywhere from three to five grocery bills per *week*, depending on how many different vendors he uses. So at the end of the month, he winds up with a stack of bills, mainly from your company and people like you. It's human nature for a person to say, "Look at all these bills! These prices are killing me!" because to the eye, physically, they are in greater number. But that is not your fault. He needs your products as much as he needs someone to cook them and the roof over his head. So what's he going to do?

> **NOTE**
>
> If the owner is broke every month, it's easy to blame it on the groceries. After all, there are more of *those* bills, so they must be the culprit. Again, if you get the owner to look at the totality of monthly expenses, that person may discover he or she is in a lease that's too expensive or has too many people on the clock.

For several years, we maintained a buying relationship with a company whose prices weren't the lowest in town because we liked the rep. He was friendly and knowledgeable. He offered useful suggestions for our menu. Occasionally, he'd stop by for lunch, even bringing other people with him so they could try our place out. He wasn't too pushy and never overstayed his welcome on sales calls. He knew his company wasn't the cheapest in town, but he stood by his brand anyway. He'd give us his best price on several items, but counterbalance that by offering price adjustments on others. He explained that he worked on commission and had to make a living, so at least he was honest. He got us set up with rebate programs. And he *always* answered his phone or personally delivered something we needed in a pinch. He did all he could within his power and within the parameters that made financial sense to his livelihood to earn our business…and he earned it for several years.

> **NOTE**
>
> If the food costs *are* too high but other metrics are within acceptable levels, then the restaurant simply needs to raise its prices.

Chapter 18: If You Sell to Foodservice People...

Interview with Corey Smith, District Manager for a Major Broadline Supplier

How long have you been around the foodservice industry? What's your background?

For 30 years. I started working at a cheesesteak franchise when I was 15. I've been a doorman, bouncer, and waiter, and later a restaurant manager and corporate trainer. The last 10 years I've worked for a broadline supplier, where I'm now a district manager.

What differences do you notice between successful accounts and those who struggle?

The best accounts pay COD, EFT (Electronic Funds Transfer). These same accounts normally have strong inventory control practices, use an order guide, have daily sales logs, manage their labor effectively, and are working owners.

I'm starting a new catering business or restaurant. What should I look for when comparing food vendors like yourself?

You should look for a vendor that is a broadliner, reaching multiple areas of your business—a one-stop shop, if you will. U.S. Foods, Sysco etc. You can purchase dairy, produce, meats, dry grocery, frozen foods, beverages, chemicals, disposables, and equipment. Have a specialty vendor as a backup for special events. Make sure the vendor has the quality of products and services that support your business—products that you'll be proud to build your business with and the capability of helping you stay ahead of industry trends.

Some vendors offer cash and/or rebates if you select them as your primary supplier. How does that work?

Think of it like a casino. A casino will give you hotel stay, food coupons, and free drinks, all to entice you to gamble at their casino. The goal is to get you to spend your money with them. It is a give-to-get proposition. Food distributors make money moving cases. The more you buy, the better likelihood they'll recoup their investment in your business.

How do you make money off me, the operator?

I make money two ways. One way is by moving large quantities of product. I can sell you your high-volume items at a lower price because the volume justifies it. Other items that aren't big movers are sold at a slightly higher margin to generate commission dollars.

Who are the primary decision-makers you deal with?

Primarily the owner. Secondarily the chef. Truthfully, you want to have a relationship with the person who pays the bills. The person ordering takes orders from the person paying the bills, the owner.

What's the ideal relationship with an account?

An ideal relationship is based on trust—trust that is earned through demonstrating you are the go-to person with the best-quality products at a competitive price.

What are some things that will make life easy for both of us?

If everyone is organized, truthful, and eager to have open communication.

Other than selling me food, what other services do you offer the restaurant operator?

I offer menu analysis, menu profit analysis, mobile ordering, sales consultants, recipe development, on-demand business analytics, use of a state-of-the art commercial test kitchen, marketing support, and manufacturer rebates. But there are others. For example, let's say I have fresh chicken with 13 days left on the dating. Unless someone buys it, we will freeze it at 9 a.m. I may come to you and let you know when there are situations like that. If you have a special event or want to run a special, I can sell it to you for, say, $60 a case instead of $75 or whatever it may be. The product is perfectly fine and everybody wins.

What advice can you give people new to the business?

Do your homework. Know who your customer is, the demographics of your area, what price point your market will bear, your fixed costs. Negotiate well if you are leasing. This is an emotional business. People work with their emotions. They cook with their emotions. It's easy to take things personally, but it's not personal. Save money wherever you can.

Chapter 19

To My Fellow Americans...

Here in America, we buy stuff. Whether we can afford it or not, that's what we do. This country revolves around debits and credits, not good deeds and fairness—and certainly not "how things should be." Thankfully, there are kind-hearted people who look out for those who can't look out for themselves. But for the able-bodied, no mercy is shown.

So who has it the hardest in America? Who gets fucked with the most? I'll tell you: The poor get fucked with. The uneducated get fucked with. More precisely, people who don't own anything get fucked with. If you don't own anything, you don't have any leverage. And leverage—or power, if you prefer—is what gets you the fairest shake in this country. Without leverage or power, you can't negotiate a better deal for yourself.

The Power of Ownership

Although it looks that way, leverage and power are not reserved solely for the wealthy. If you're an average bootstrapper like the majority of us, the easiest way to obtain leverage or power is ownership. Owners make the rules. Owners make the decisions. Owners get listened to. If all you are is a perpetual consumer, you accept what is offered and do as you are told. If you want the greatest breadth and quality of choices, at some point ownership is necessary. In other words, the best defense against a life of financial struggle in the country that arguably offers the greatest potential to improve one's situation is a good offense. America's construct favors ownership and in the long run, ownership is what will benefit you the most—owning the home in which you live, owning the job that makes you a living. Anytime you lease, borrow, or work for anything owned by someone else, it can be taken away.

The easiest path to ownership is to first take ownership of yourself. If you think of yourself as a brand, what are your features and benefits? What is your value proposition? How can you apply it to an entrepreneurial pursuit? As for me, my value proposition is I have a macro view of the broader potential and an unwavering dedication to the task at hand. Erin, on the other hand, excels on the micro side of things—planning, management, and administrative details. She's designed the layout for every business we've had, always squeezing out the maximum return. She can walk into a space with a tape measure—no paper or pen—go home, and from memory draw a floor plan of where everything needs to go, kitchen and dining room. The bottom line, everyone has some tangibles. You've used your skills and talents working for someone else and been paid what they think you're worth. Why not use those same skills on something you dream up?

> **NOTE**
>
> There is often talk about the imminent demise of the middle class. Some say in the future, there will only be two classes: the ownership class and the people who serve them. Being in the service class is perfectly fine, but it's better if you *own* the service. This of course shifts you to the ownership class. Think about it: Wouldn't you rather own the janitorial service, restaurant, call center, or warehouse than work there? You can also own an idea. Look at companies like Uber and Airbnb. They figured out how to own a service without having to own the hard assets—i.e., the vehicles and real estate.

The American Dream

I enjoy bumping into other operators at auctions or warehouses and talking shop. I learn so much from them. I especially like to hear stories about their businesses and how they've maintained them as long as they have. Some of them are first-generation immigrants who opened a restaurant when they arrived in this country and it's still open after 20 or 30 years. They love talking about business—how this or that deal is in the works or what property they're looking to buy to start up a new idea.

These people inspire me. They've embraced the spirit of America. Some came to this country from places where people without power or leverage are fucked with even more than they are here in the States. Their attitude is, they'll be *damned* if they're going to come all the way here and be fucked with some more. Do they experience racism and classism? Sure. But they realize that the people who perpetuate it are inconsequential to their plans. They laugh at the way we Americans act and the time we waste. They know what's great about this country, and why so many people risk their lives to get here: the money and the freedom—the fact you can gain your own little piece of power.

Chapter 19: To My Fellow Americans...

The people I'm talking about come from all over the world: Asia, Africa, Latin America, the Middle East, and Europe. Regardless of where they're from, they all express one common theme: They know in America, it's possible to get that leverage. They also know just about everything is a math problem. Numbers either work or they don't, in any language or country. Math is the constant.

How do they start with so little and do so well in such a short time? After being in the industry long enough, and being married to a person who's from another land, I've seen it happen over and over. Almost to a person, it goes like this: The couple arrives in America. Let's say the wife is 25, the husband is 30, and they have two kids under the age of five. They've managed to save or borrow a few thousand bucks, and that's all they have to their name.

The first year they're here, they find an affordable apartment and furnish it modestly with items from consignment stores, thrift shops, or a church ministry. They buy an old but reliable car. They find cheap child care for the children. Eventually, when they're a little older, they'll enroll them in the local public school. (A free education through 12th grade? Hell yeah!) The husband gets a job wherever he can—at a warehouse, as a laborer, or in a kitchen. The wife also gets a job—full or part time—usually in retail or foodservice or at a bank. (Math is universal, remember?) They cook at home. Their clothes are from big box stores—Target, Wal-Mart, or what have you—or, like their furniture, second-hand.

During years two through five, they save enough money for a down payment on a house, so they buy one. They add another reliable vehicle to the household. Both the husband and the wife are still at their jobs and have missed at most a handful of days in three or four years. By now, they might even be shift leaders or supervisors. The kids are sailing through school, making friends, and can speak perfect English in addition to their native language.

Between years five and 10, the couple has saved enough money for the husband to leave his job and start his own business. The wife still works, but part time. The husband's business could be anything from a restaurant to a flooring-installation company to a lawn-care service. Whatever it is, it's not terribly complicated and has something to do with service. The couple figures out something people want or need and will pay someone else to do—something practical. They didn't come all the way to this country with the intention of getting a job at Megapharm or IBM; they came to create jobs for themselves.

During years 10 through 15, the business explodes. The husband and wife have worked it to the bone. They've reinvested in the business but still put money aside in savings. They abhor debt. Anything they buy, they pay for in cash, and if they can't pay for it in cash, they don't need it. The kids are growing up American but have avoided a lot of bullshit. Their grades are good. When it's time to leave for college, they study IT, engineering, or medicine. There's some scholarship money coming their way and they find the best internships.

After year 15, the couple's business continues to thrive. They sell their starter home and buy or build another—no mortgage. They own several rental properties, which they bought cheap, paid for in cash, and fixed up. They've visited their home country many times, sharing stories with relatives about life in America and keeping their children in touch with their roots. The kids are finishing their education and are on to promising careers with jobs that are hard to get laid off from. Or, they are poised to become entrepreneurs like their parents. All the family cars are paid for, and they still buy everything with cash. Meals are still eaten primarily at home but they enjoy going out on special occasions. The only splurge has been a condo in Florida their daughter talked them into buying. It, of course, has no mortgage either. Our hard-working couple doesn't have to work so hard anymore. And because they're not even 50 years old, they'll go on to enjoy their own little kingdom and the freedom that comes with it for many years to come. They're *owners*.

Keep in mind for people like our couple here, English was their second language. And because they looked a little different, odds are they had to navigate some bigotry. But these people got hip real quick to the fact it can get you sidetracked, and they didn't bite. From the start, they've known one thing: All they had to do was figure out the math problem. Has everything been perfect for these people? No. Surely there were tough times and setbacks. But this is how it goes down. You are free to disagree with anything you've read in this book thus far, but please don't debate me on this example. I know what I'm talking about here and have seen it with my own eyes.

So why did I go into all this? Because I want those of you who were born here, who were schooled here, and who know the lay of the land to think about that couple when you get exasperated from the grind. They made it, and didn't start with *half* of what we start with.

Chapter 20

Leftovers

Enjoying the Challenge

I fall in and out of love with what I do, but I never stop thinking about it. The risks, the long hours, and the multitude of people needed for it to function leave me exhausted at times. But to see it all come together and work is a feeling like no other.

I think the reason it continuously intrigues me is because it's so challenging…and in the end, I love the challenge. I always prefer challenge to competition. To me, a challenge involves using will and determination to overcome an obstacle and accomplish a goal. A competition, on the other hand, is a contest, with the end result of a winner and a loser. Sometimes I'll win and sometimes I'll lose, but I get a bigger rush from the challenge. If I get through the challenge, I've won the battle with myself.

Snobbery

Is there snobbery among peers? I'm sure there is—although anybody in this industry has a lot of nerve looking down their nose at another operator, knowing how hard it is to succeed. If a corner rib joint has been open the same 40 years as an urbane city bistro, I'd say the community agrees they're both playing at the same level.

My experience meeting other owners is there's generally a feeling of mutual respect. The respect is there because at some point in our careers, we've assuredly gone through a mutual hell only we would understand. Our concepts may be wildly different, but at the end of the day, we're doing the same thing: feeding people.

Besides, it's just cooking. If you can follow a recipe, with a little practice, you can cook anything. What's the difference between a medium-rare burger and a medium-rare steak? $30. Cooks from gourmet restaurants leave to paint houses for a few years, then come back and sauté quail. None of us care what's on the other person's menu. It's only what we have in common that carries any real significance: whether we are *open* or *closed*.

> **NOTE**
> Any snobbery I've encountered usually comes from people on the periphery. Of course, everyone's entitled to their opinion. But it doesn't mean I have to care about it.

Making Do in Flyover Country

Let's face it. If you live anywhere in the U.S. other than the East Coast or the West Coast, America and the rest of the world really isn't checking for you, culturally speaking. You're in flyover country. (I love you, Chicago. But that includes you, too.) Other than certain hallowed events and city traditions that occasionally make the news, for the most part, we're ignored. It's understandable. New York is rich, powerful, global and expensive. Sexy California is spacious, sunny, and eccentric.

But just because the next hip thing being forced on the public is from California or New York doesn't mean any of it is gospel. Like everywhere else, restaurants open and close every day and Monopoly money and Honeycomb Hideouts number in the thousands instead of the hundreds.

If you're in flyover country, like I am, take your own risks and express yourself anyway you want! I mean, if I were to serve tempura-battered tamales filled with traditional American soul food from a rickshaw here in the Midwest I'd be taken as an oddity—someone who's trying too hard. But if I did the same thing in California or New York, you'd get sick of seeing me on TV. That's just how things are.

It's always funny when people come in and say, "Hey! I'm from San Francisco"—or New York or L.A. or wherever—"and your food wasn't too bad!" I thank them for their visit and kind words. But I admit that I *really* want to say, "What does that mean? What am I supposed to do with that information, exactly?" We've eaten plenty of meals in New York and California, and like most places you go, some were good, some sucked, and the rest were in the middle. The only real difference was that the owner's rent was probably three times what we pay in Indiana. (I will say, however, I've never had a bad meal in New Orleans.) I just figure, next time I'm at a restaurant in *their* city, I'll make it a point to say I'm from Indianapolis and to note how impressed I was with *their* efforts.

Chapter 20: Leftovers

Our Indy

Welcome to Indianapolis, the city settled by people on their way to Chicago but ran out of money. Nothing's open past 2 a.m. but White Castle and legs. We've heard all the jokes—and we don't mind poking fun at ourselves, either.

Admittedly, our contribution to the historical narrative of this country is fairly thin. Off the cuff, it's hard to quickly pinpoint something—anything—about Indianapolis that sticks in the brain (except maybe the Colts, Pacers, and Indianapolis 500). Still, we like to remind ourselves (and anyone within earshot) that we are alive and breathing. This is sometimes evidenced by local media referencing each and every Hoosier connection to anything, anywhere. B-list celebrity sightings and their opinion of our town are also hot topics for discussion. We love attention when we can get it.

But when you get past the mostly flat, landlocked geography, the harsh winters, occasional headlines related to some sort of archaic legislation, and jabs from travelers at our nanny-state blue laws, it's actually a great place to live. There are wonderful people here—down-to-earth, intelligent people with a sense a humor. We get along fairly well, have our share of fine women, and there is plenty of soul.

What people in some cities pay for a two-bedroom apartment will allow ownership of a downtown condo with a view or a Frank Lloyd Wright–inspired Mid Century home jutting from a hillside in the woods. You can maintain a savings account here. That means there's money left over to travel if you need a quick getaway. We're a day or less by car to half of the U.S., and with exception of the West Coast, no more than a couple hours by plane.

As for setting up a restaurant here, the good news is you don't choke on much red tape. Key people are generally accessible. And yes, people here can cook. Obviously, we aren't on a coast, so your seafood expectations should fall in line. But we have dedicated fish markets who can deliver on any promise with top-quality product. Besides, what we lack in ocean fare we more than make up for with the farms, fields, forests, and orchards less than an hour away in any direction. We make some great beer, too.

There's no shortage of talent or creativity in Indianapolis. Our biggest challenge, in my opinion, is the audience. Great food scenes are built, but only if the locals buy in. The more support the scene gets, the more places open. More places means more choices. When people support new choices, intrepid owners and chefs feel confident investing time and money to open yet more places. So the job ahead is to continuously win over new diners.

While we have a population of just a million or so people, we are known as one of the best performing metros when it comes to chain restaurants with hearty fare. Here in Indy, we like to eat until we get full. That's who we are. Convincing people to take a break from the buffets can be tough, but more and more folks are foregoing the hype and revisiting the neighborhood restaurant down the street. As our citizenry buys into the talent of honest local efforts and support unconventional locations and neighborhoods, the sky will be the limit for our food scene.

Cooking for Fun

For me, cooking has always been therapeutic. That's probably because it's just me and the ingredients (and if I am lucky, some fun people to be around). You can make food do whatever you want it to—in other words, tomatoes don't talk back!

Our family eats fairly simply at home. We keep plenty of fruit around and usually take turns cooking. Erin loves experimenting with new recipes but still holds firmly onto her family dishes from Egypt. On rainy days, if we're lying around the house, Erin likes her wine, and we'll nibble on her favorite snack of dried bread, olives, and feta cheese. As for me, I'll cook whatever, but my favorite is breakfast food. Sometimes, though, I like to go a little crazy. I'll spend a week planning and writing down ideas. I'll think about the meal while I'm in the shower or driving around, imagining that first bite. Finally, I'll go to two or three different stores to get everything I need. Then, with all the ingredients in place, I'll set up the kitchen, put on some music, relax, and start cooking.

For me, one of the most precious times while our kids were growing up was watching them pick up their little spoons and forks, seeing them navigate their bowl or plate. Getting their reactions to new foods was always amusing, then and now. Hearing them and their friends describe what they like and don't like is a hoot. They're so honest. We've shared so many moments at the table with family and friends, with food being the glue that's brought us together.

Our Wish for You

We've gone over how easy—and yet how tough—foodservice is. You've read about the critical thinking required after you've made the choice to accept the personal and financial commitment to start your own foodservice business. You know not to rush into concept ideas and signing leases without doing your homework, crunching the numbers, and making a plan, even if it takes a couple of years. You'll open your doors to share your version of our most basic needs, food and drink. You'll create a gathering

Chapter 20: Leftovers

place in your corner of the world where memories will be made for you and your guests. There is no greater joy than seeing this play out in front of you, in your "house."

You understand that to survive as a business owner, you must respect the fundamentals. That's the only way you and your guests will be able to enjoy your business for as long as it's meant to be. You accept the fact that if you're starting any business, restaurant or not, there will be periods of discomfort, especially in the beginning. These will stabilize, however. If you keep going, there will be a light at the end of the tunnel.

There's no governing board in foodservice. There are very few meddlesome hoops to jump through. Apart from requirements set by the health department and fire marshal, you are unrestricted. You are free to cook what you want, how you want. You can deliver it to your guest as creatively as you like and charge any amount of money you wish. You can play in one of the last unmolested segments in business and the market will decide your success or failure. That's why foodservice so intriguing. It's one of the purest forms of commerce.

If you've done your best and things don't work out, don't be discouraged. After a taste of this business, you are officially prepared for anything that may come next—including *another* taste of this business. If you want more, don't worry. The foodservice industry isn't going anywhere!

What's next for us? I don't know. We'll exercise an upcoming option to renew our lease. Our trusty idea binders are stuffed full with info for two concepts we've been working on. One's about 80% completed, the other about 50%. It's possible we'll give them a try down the road. Maybe, if we follow our own advice, they'll make a little money—or, not. We'll see.

At any rate, that's all for now. But there is certainly much more to talk about, and there are definitely more stories. Let's keep in touch at www.RestaurantWinners.com.

We wish you the best, and can't wait to visit your place. Be bold. Be fearless. Above all, keep pushing.

Cheers.

www.ingramcontent.com/pod-product-compliance
Lightning Source LLC
Chambersburg PA
CBHW081355290426
44110CB00018B/2386